# *Success* Signals

## RHONDA HILYER

**THIRD EDITION**

**Published by Agreement Dynamics, Inc.**
**PO Box 33640**
**Seattle, WA 98133**
**(206) 546-8048**

FOR ADDITIONAL INFORMATION
ON AGREEMENT DYNAMICS
PLEASE CALL: 1-800-97-AGREE

OR EMAIL YOUR INQUIRY TO:
hq@agreementdynamics.com

Printed in the USA
Third Edition

Book layout by Ginny Ratliff

ISBN 0-9710258-0-0
Library of Congress Control Number: 2001095696

This book is dedicated to Ginny Ratliff and Dee Endelman with deep appreciation for their important contributions to *Success Signals* and their ongoing support, love of laughter and professional excellence.

# Contents

# 1

# Introduction to the Signals of Success

Every one of us has a unique way of expressing our thoughts, feelings and beliefs. We all develop preferences and tendencies toward certain words, phrases, volume, pitch, pace, body language and other signals to send our messages. The preferred set of signals that each of us uses is known as our "style" of communication. It's not "what" we're trying to get across, but "how."

All styles are valuable and important. Whatever your style, you can use it effectively or ineffectively. Studies show that 80 percent of those who fail at work do so for one reason:

**"THEY DO NOT RELATE OR
COMMUNICATE WELL WITH OTHERS."**

How we use our communication style—and the signals associated with it—is often the strongest determinant of our success or failure in attaining both the results and relationships we desire.

Learning to use the signals of your style effectively will not only improve virtually all your relationships, it will enable you to dramatically increase your ability to persuade others to be more receptive to you and your message.

> *"The greatest skill needed for success is the ability to get along with other people. It impacts every part of a person's life. Your relationships make you or break you."*
>
> **– JOHN C. MAXWELL**

What exactly are these signals that we use to communicate information, ideas, needs, wants or feelings to others?

The signals we send include:

- Tone of voice
- Volume (loudness/softness of speech)
- Speed (how quickly or slowly you speak)
- Pitch (how high or low your voice is)
- Inflection
- Accent
- Facial expressions
- Gestures
- Movement
- Proximity (how close you stand)
- Energy level
- Use of humor
- Eye contact
- Cleanliness
- Hair
- Fingernails
- Jewelry
- Clothing
- Fragrance/smell—both type and strength
- Make-up

When you are talking to another person or to a group, you are sending about 15 to 20 of these communication signals in addition to the words you are saying.

Although words are important, studies show that they only count for about 7 percent of the interpretation of the speaker's message. So when others are trying to determine what you are saying and whether they should believe you, other signals (in addition to words) are often powerful influencers.

SOME SIGNALS WE SEND INCLUDE:

*Volume (loudness of speech)*

*Facial expressions*

*Gestures*

*Clothing*

Added to this, research indicates that when you are talking to another person or group of people, you lose their attention at least every 30 seconds (sometimes even more).

This is true no matter how engaging a speaker you are or how interesting the topic is. Cognitive scientists (who study how our brains work) tell us that we are hardwired to have intruding thoughts continuously, with no more than 30 seconds elapsed.

So if you have trouble communicating sometimes, welcome to the human race. We all have trouble communicating. The key is to first become aware of "how" we tend to send our messages (the signals we send) as well as how others are likely to interpret our set of signals or style of communication.

> YOUR COMMUNICATION STYLE IS NOT *WHAT* YOU SAY BUT *HOW* YOU SAY IT.

## COMMUNICATION STYLE — WHAT IS IT?

Again, communication style is not *what* you say but *how* you say it.

We all know people who get to the bottom line right away, no chitchat. We know other people who like to share stories and jokes before they get to the point. They may gesture boldly, and vary the pitch and volume of their speech dramatically while others speak quietly or in a monotone.

Some folks are sequential and linear in their speech. Others jump all around.

Some of us talk a lot about feelings, and laugh, cry or hug more often when we communicate. Others speak in objective, factual, non-emotional terms and appear more reserved.

Some of us exaggerate for effect; others send and receive messages very literally.

We all may be trying to say the same thing...but we say it in such different ways!

We each have our own unique style of communication.

## SO WHAT?

Here's the problem. We humans seek to understand intent as well as information. We make meaning out of what we observe.

When we observe a person's communication style, we receive and interpret the signals they send.

And we start to draw conclusions about the inner person. About their:

- Hopes
- Dreams
- Fears
- Spirit
- Beliefs
- Values
- Motivations

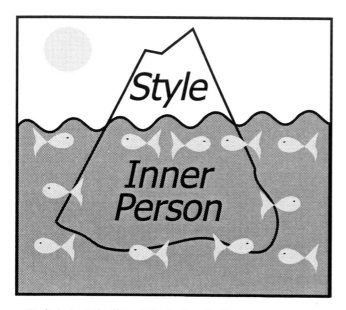

*Style is just the "tip of the iceberg" of human personality.*

We form our impression of the inner person based largely on style.

And, if their style is very different from ours, we sometimes form a *bad* impression.

We misunderstand one another.

We misinterpret what is said or what is intended or both.

We start to judge the person based on *how* they are saying things, more than on *what they are actually saying.*

And this leads to...you guessed it — *conflict!*

The good news is that CONFLICT BASED ON STYLE IS LARGELY AVOIDABLE.

Would you like to reduce the level of needless conflict in your life?

Would you like to send clear and successful signals to others?

Would you like to understand that other person in your life—your partner, your child, your boss, your friend—better?

Would you like others to understand you better and be more receptive to your message?

## CONCLUSION:

Understanding communication styles and the signals associated with them is like learning a language. When you understand the language of style, you can be successful in communicating with most people you meet. When you understand the signals of others and when you communicate in ways that get your intended message across, YOU SEND SUCCESS SIGNALS. People will find you easy to talk to and they will listen to you. That's communication success!

Understanding your unique communication style is the first step toward sending success signals.

> WHEN YOU UNDERSTAND THE SIGNALS OF OTHERS AND WHEN YOU COMMUNICATE IN WAYS THAT GET YOUR INTENDED MESSAGE ACROSS, YOU SEND SUCCESS SIGNALS.

# NOTES

# 2

# The Success Signals System:
# The "Colors" of Success

W e've been interested in style for a long time. Since ancient times, human beings have studied themselves and their fellow beings. We have always wanted to know how the human personality works. Theories about our individual communication styles go back at least to the ancient Greeks.

They believed that people had dominant "temperaments." Philosophers described humans as being made up primarily of one of the four basic elements: *air, water, fire* or *earth.* Your way of acting in the world (that is, your *style*) depended on which of these four elements controlled you.

As the fields of psychology and social science emerged during the 20th century, we developed numerous models designed to help us understand human behavior, including the Meyers-Briggs Inventory, Performax, the Keirsey/Bates Model, the FIRO-B Inventory, the Strategic Deployment Inventory and many more.

> *"Communication. It is not only the essence of being human but also a vital property of life."*
>
> *- John A. Pierce*

# THE SUCCESS SIGNALS "COLORS"

The colors system of communication was inspired by the work of Stefan Neilson and Shay Thoelke. Stephan and Shay—a psychologist and an art teacher—drew on numerous behavioral models to develop the first generation of color cards. In addition to the behavioral modification work of B. F. Skinner, these behavioral practitioners used the principles of Neurolinguistics, Rorschach Testing, the Learning Styles System, Rotter's Locus of Control and other research methods.

The result was a simple tool to better understand your unique communication style.

Using the original color cards, this author developed the "Success Signals" System along with the internationally field-tested "Colors of Success" seminar. This program is unique, having several benefits not found in any other "styles" models. For example,

- It is multidimensional. Participants use words, symbols and colors to identify their unique communication style. As a result, accuracy tends to be higher.

- Colors are more neutral than words. There is less judgment attached to styles when they are identified by color.

- Because communication styles are presented as "blends" of four colors, there is less stereotyping. People do not tend to pigeonhole themselves or others into artificial boxes as often as they do with other models.

- Communication styles by colors and symbols is faster and easier to learn than strictly word-based methods.

> BECAUSE COMMUNICATION STYLES ARE PRESENTED AS "BLENDS" OF FOUR COLORS, THERE IS LESS STEREOTYPING.

- Communication styles by color and symbols is hard to forget. It sticks with participants almost effortlessly.
- Communication styles by colors and symbols is both simple and complex. As a result, it appeals to all ages, cultures, professions and educational levels.
- Communication styles by colors and symbols is FUN! It is so enjoyable and engaging, participants are energized by the learning experience.
- Communication styles by colors has a great track record as a primary tool for successful conflict resolution, negotiation, team building, collaborative problem solving, improved customer service, sales and enhanced personal relationships.

THE ORDER OF YOUR COLOR CARDS DEPICTS YOUR UNIQUE COMMUNICATION STYLE BLEND.

## SORTING YOUR "COLORS": A SELF-ASSESSMENT

In the back of this book are four cards. Each card is a different color, and each card has a different graphic design with special symbols as well as different words on the front. On the back is a more detailed description.

Do a brief self-assessment to help you understand *your* unique style.

Following are instructions for this self-assessment:

1. Look at the front of each card (the side with the large symbols). Observe the color, design and the words. Do not read the backs of the cards, yet.

2. As you look at each card, notice which ones seem really like you. This should be an intuitive response so don't spend too much time thinking about each card.

3. Ask yourself the question, "Which of these cards is most like me most of the time?" Put that card on top.

4. Ask yourself, "Which of these cards is *second* most like me? *Third?* Which card is the *least* like me?"

5. Rank the cards in order. Put the one you think is most like you *most of the time* on top. Put the one that you think is least like you on the bottom.

6. Give yourself no more than TWO MINUTES to do this exercise. Yes, you *can* do it in two minutes!

When you read the front of the cards, you may hesitate. You may think to yourself, "Well, sometimes I'm like this card and sometimes I'm like another one." That's true. We are all a blend of all four styles, a unique blend. Nevertheless, put the cards in rank order to the best of your ability.

**RANK ORDER YOUR CARDS NOW.**

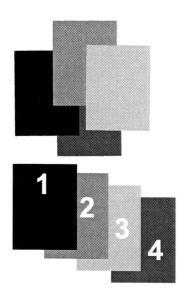

*Place the card most like you most of the time on top.*

*Place the card that is second most like you next.*

*Place the card that is third most like you next.*

*Place the card that is least like you on the bottom.*

YOUR CARD ORDER DETERMINES YOUR UNIQUE COMMUNICATION STYLE.

# Learning the Primary Language of Each Color

We are now going to give you a basic description of each color "language."

First, here's a warning:

> THE FOLLOWING DESCRIPTIONS WILL BE SIMPLISTIC. REMEMBER THAT NONE OF US IS PURE. (THAT SHOULD BE EASY TO REMEMBER.) WE ARE ALL A COMPLEX BLEND OF THESE FOUR STYLES AND THE SIGNALS THAT WE SEND ARE USUALLY NOT AS SIMPLE AS THEY SEEM HERE.

"LET'S WORK TOGETHER"

# THE BLUE STYLE

If you put the Blue card on top, you may find that you:

- Can get the "feel" of a crowd of people the minute you walk into a room;
- Know the morale level in your work place;
- Are privy to all the latest buzz on the changes coming down in your organization; and
- Are called upon by others as a "shoulder to cry on."

There are two reasons for this.

1. The Blue style is more sensitive to human emotion than any other style. They easily "read" subtle emotional and non-verbal signals (such as body language, energy level, tone, eye contact) that others send; and

2. Blue style communicators are often great listeners. So people talk to them. They share information freely, knowing that they will get an open and sympathetic ear.

To the Blue style, the main purpose of communication is to *connect with other people*.

Blue style communicators tend to send communication signals that are:

- People oriented
- Sensitive
- Supportive
- Considerate
- Relationship building

Let's explore these in a little more detail.

## MAKING DECISIONS

Blue style communicators tend to make decisions based on people first, facts second. This is not to say that they *ignore* facts but that facts are less important to them than questions such as:

- How will this decision impact others?
- Have I consulted with people in making this decision?
- Who is likely to be happy/upset with this decision?

## CONFLICT

Blue style communicators do not like conflict. Why? Because, for a *Blue*, each interaction is woven into the fabric of the relationship and *conflict* is seen as a negative interaction that tears at this fabric.

Does that mean that these folks never get angry, that they're wimps and can be run over? Absolutely not!

The signals a *Blue* will tend to send in conflict situations are:

- Silence. They just "clam up."
- Indirect responses. Rather than confront the conflict, *Blues* will send subtle signals that something is wrong. For example, if you are playing music too loud, a Blue style communicator might say, "Do you really like listening to loud rock music?" rather than, "That's too loud. Please turn it down!" (You see, if you asked a *Blue* that same question, they would take your subtle cue and ask, "Oh, is my music too loud for you?" They expect others to do the same and are some times seriously disappointed on this one.)
- Seeming compliance. They "go by the book." It may be, however, "malicious compliance," following an order to the letter and in a way that causes problems.

> TO THE BLUE STYLE, THE MAIN PURPOSE OF COMMUNICATION IS TO *CONNECT WITH OTHER PEOPLE.*

- Martyrdom. *Blues* may silently look up to heaven or let out a big sigh. "Oh, what we have to put up with!"

The *Blues* may try to avoid conflict but, they don't easily forget a conflict. Their motto is "Give in and get even!" More about this later.

## LANGUAGE

Blue style communicators speak in the language of *feelings*. They like people to tell them about their "true feelings." They are more likely to ask you how you feel about something, rather than what you *think* about it.

And they want everyone to get along, to work together. A typical *Blue* statement is: "Can't we all just get along?"

## HOW *BLUES* ARE MISUNDERSTOOD:

Sometimes *Blues* are seen as weak or wimpy because they don't usually scream or pound the table. *Blues* as a group are just as strong and stubborn as anyone else is. Individual *Blues* may be strong or weak, just as individual *Reds*, *Greens* or *Browns* are. It's important not to stereotype styles.

Sometimes perceived as always wanting to socialize and bond with people rather than get things done, *Blues* believe that more is accomplished when people understand and support each other.

## OVERALL

Helen Keller summed up the Blue style perspective eloquently when she wrote: "Alone we can do so little, together we can do so much."

We all have some Blue in our style and it's a good thing. Otherwise, our relationships would be missing that sense of human connection that keeps them vital, positive and productive.

> BLUE STYLE COMMUNICATORS SPEAK IN THE LANGUAGE OF *FEELINGS*.

# THE BROWN STYLE

"JUST DO IT!"

If you put the Brown card on top, you've probably skimmed this book looking for a summary of its contents. After all, why waste time? Let's just get to the point and move on. "I've got a lot to do."

To a Brown style communicator, the purpose of communication is to *get things done!*

Brown style communicators are task focused and results oriented. They don't want you to tell them that they are "nice people." They would rather hear: "Keep up the good work."

Brown style communicators send signals that are:
- Decisive
- Direct
- Action focused
- Authoritative
- Bottom-line oriented

## DECISION MAKING

Remember that Blue style communicators make decisions based on people first, facts second. Brown style communicators prefer facts but do not necessarily need much information to make a decision. They make them without hesitating.

And, if they make a mistake, they know that they can just make a mid-course correction and move on. In other words, if a Brown style communicator makes a decision that isn't working…they just make another decision to correct it.

## CONFLICT

Conflict is sometimes a means to resolve things for the Brown style communicator. Some people think they might even *like* conflict from the signals they send when entering into it—strong, unafraid and even letting their anger show. But many *Browns* will tell you that they don't either like or dislike conflict. It is just a fact of life, a way to get off the dime, bring things to a head and move on.

One of the reasons that *Browns* don't mind conflict is their ability to compartmentalize. They have a well-developed sense of boundaries. So two Brown-style communicators can have a loud argument at work and then go out to lunch together. This really confuses their friends of the Blue style. However, from the *Brown* perspective, "That was work and this is social."

In conflict, *Browns* tend to send signals that are:

- Direct and blunt—unlike their more indirect *Blue* colleagues, you know when you are fighting with a *Brown*.
- Unilateral—often makes demands or issues ultimatums.
- Angry—if the conflict raises their ire, they'll show it.

## LANGUAGE

Brown style communicators speak in the language of *commands*. They tell rather than ask. They like short statements and direct questions. When they hear the word "no," they think it means "maybe." So when they say, "no," they expect you to come back with more information or a different argument if you are strongly committed to your idea.

You know someone is speaking *Brown* when they say things like: "What's the bottom line?" "Cut to the chase." or "Stop whining!"

## HOW *BROWNS* ARE MISUNDERSTOOD:

Because they are blunt and direct, *Browns* are sometimes perceived by others to be rude, insensitive and

> TO A
> BROWN STYLE
> COMMUNICATOR,
> THE PURPOSE OF
> COMMUNICATION
> IS TO *GET*
> *THINGS DONE!*

uncaring. Not so. They think their straight talk makes it easier for others to understand them. Also, because *Browns* sometimes talk in commands (and are unaware of it), e.g., "Get me some coffee, Sue," they are perceived as dictatorial, controlling and/or rigid. *Browns* — as a group — are no more dictatorial or rigid than other styles in their intentions. There are just as many *Blues*, *Reds* and *Greens* who can be dictatorial and rigid. *Browns* are often so focused on getting things done that they don't always see how they are coming across. They are often the ones who organize efforts to help others and work hard to make sure people aren't laid off, but they rarely tell others what they've done.

## OVERALL

The Brown style is summed up in Lee Iacocca's famous saying, "Lead, follow or get out of the way." We all have some Brown in our style and that's a good thing. Otherwise, we would not accomplish much and certainly not in *real time*.

> BROWN STYLE COMMUNICATORS SPEAK IN THE LANGUAGE OF *COMMANDS*. THEY TELL RATHER THAN ASK.

"LOOK BEFORE YOU LEAP"

# THE GREEN STYLE

If you put the Green card on top, you have probably been wondering whether we have the facts, research and data to back up this theory of style. "Success signals, indeed" you might be thinking. "Where is the research?" (It is for your benefit that we have additional information in the back of this book, including a reading list.)

To the Green style, the purpose of communication is to *exchange information.*

Green style communicators send signals that are:

- Logical
- Factual
- Analytical
- Thorough

## DECISION MAKING

Green style communicators don't just want to make a decision. They want to make the *right* decision. Accordingly, they place a high value on facts, logic, research and data. Because they need to carefully analyze the data, put it into its proper context, interpret the research and reach reasoned conclusions...this style is the *slowest* decision-maker.

Green style communicators also tend to be the most skeptical and perfectionistic of all the styles. They are focused on quality and accuracy. They like to get things done right the first time. So, when you want a *Green* to make a decision:

1. Make sure you have "done your homework";
2. Give details, not just the "bottom line";
3. Make sure she has enough time to consider the information; and
4. Don't expect an instant answer.

And, if you want to destabilize your relationship with a Green style communicator, just give him some new information right before an important decision deadline!

## CONFLICT

Green style communicators tend to depersonalize conflict. That doesn't mean that they never get their feelings hurt. It *does* mean that they will not usually react to conflict situations right away. They will process the situation to determine whether you "done them wrong" before they respond.

In conflict, Green style communicators tend to send signals that are:

- Indirect—they will not spark conflict. When confronted, they may just listen and say, "Let me think about that." And they will. (Admit it, Green style communicators, you may even make a chart analyzing the points of conflict.)
- Low key—they will not show much emotion. This does not mean that they are not feeling hurt, frustrated or angry, however.
- Quiet—Green style communicators tend to act withdrawn when they are in conflict.

Caution: This does not mean that a *Green* will not get back at you if he's hurt. It may take three days, three weeks or three years for the Green style communicator to decide that you have done him wrong but, when he does, he will meticulously plan his revenge.

> TO THE GREEN STYLE, THE PURPOSE OF COMMUNICATION IS TO *EXCHANGE INFORMATION*.

## LANGUAGE

*Greens* are very literal users of language. They eschew hyperbole and do not trust testimonials or stories as any kind of "proof." Their use of language is precise and moderate. Numbers and facts, after all, speak for themselves. This has caused some people to call them "bean counters" and "nitpickers." Actually, they can be very big-picture, innovative thinkers. They just value accuracy and organization, in communication as in all else.

You know someone is speaking Green when they say things like:

"What's the research on that?"

"In what context are you speaking?"

"Let's be reasonable."

> *GREENS* TEND TO BE THE MOST SKEPTICAL AND PERFECTIONISTIC OF ALL THE STYLES. THEY LIKE TO GET THINGS DONE RIGHT THE FIRST TIME.

## HOW *GREENS* ARE MISUNDERSTOOD:

Because *Greens* often appear serious or reserved, others sometimes assume they don't care or don't "feel" things. Not true. Just because they don't emote as readily as other styles does not mean they don't have deep feelings.

Also, *Greens* are sometimes stereotyped as "nerds" who wallow in minutia and miss the forest for the trees. Obviously some people do that, but it's the exception not the rule. Don't you want a careful, thorough, precise, accurate *Green* doing brain surgery or preparing your taxes?

## OVERALL

Ben Franklin told us that "A stitch in time saves nine." This is the *Green* credo.

We all have some Green in our style and it's a good thing because it enables us to do things *well*, preventing many mistakes, even averting disasters.

# THE RED STYLE

If you put the Red card on top, you want this book to spark ideas, be fun and motivate you to learn how to be more successful and persuasive!

Don't get too heavy with the charts and graphs...tell me why it's brilliant, creative, sexy, cool and over the top to send these Success Signals.

To the Red style, communication is not just about exchanging information but about expressing a combination of facts, feelings, drama, humor and creative ideas.

*Reds* push us beyond our self-imposed limitations. Flight is a good example. For hundreds of years people were ridiculed when they said human flight was possible. But Red style communicators weren't deterred. They had an idea—a vision—(reds tend to be visionary). As a result, the world was changed dramatically because the *Reds* were willing to risk failure and even humiliation to achieve their vision.

Red style communicators tend to send signals that are:

- Flamboyant
- Rapid fire
- Creative
- Fun loving

## DECISION MAKING

Red style communicators have absolutely no problem making a decision. They can make lots of them. In fact, they can make more decisions in five minutes than some people do in a *week!* And all on the same topic!

This has caused some people to call them "flaky." Not true. They have simply had a better idea. So what if they gave you their "decision" on the topic five minutes ago? They've had a *great idea* and now they are making another decision.

The Red style is always pushing the envelope, always looking for that new and creative way of doing things. This can result in lots of decisions in rapid-fire succession.

*Reds* rebel against too much structure. They see it as limiting creativity. They don't like rules for the sake of rules and prefer to follow the spirit rather than the letter of the law in some cases.

## CONFLICT

Red style communicators do not mind conflict. In fact, sometimes they kind of like it. It sparks creative ideas and, let's face it, a good fight can be *fun!*

In conflict, *Reds* tend to send signals that are:
- Rebellious—they'd rather fight than switch.
- Attacking—when under stress, Red style communicators can be very creative in their choice of words.
- Provocative—they say outrageous things not because they actually mean them but to vent their strong feelings in the moment.

One thing to remember about conflict with a *Red* is that when it's over, it's over. They may erupt like Mount Vesuvius but they cool quickly after a fight. For *Reds,* conflict is often a physical and emotional release.

## LANGUAGE

Red style communicators are creative in their language. They love exaggeration because it makes communication so much more interesting. These communicators are never just "cold," they're "freezing!!!" They're never just "hungry," they're "starved!!!" They consider the literal use of language boring—facts and figures mean less than testimonials, anecdotes and stories.

> RED STYLE COMMUNICATORS ARE CREATIVE IN THEIR LANGUAGE. THEY LOVE EXAGGERATION BECAUSE IT MAKES COMMUNICATION SO MUCH MORE INTERESTING!

You know someone is speaking Red when you hear multiple jokes, tall tales and highly creative use of language.

*Red* sayings include: "Trust me," "Lighten up," "Make your own kind of music," "Why be normal?"

## OVERALL

In the play *Auntie Mame,* Mame (quite a *Red* herself) sums up the *Red* philosophy of life: "Life is a banquet," she says, "and most poor suckers are starving."

Red style communicators chow down at the banquet of life!

All of us have some Red in our style and it's a good thing or we'd be stuck in a rut—not trying new things, making much progress or having fun for that matter.

> TO THE *REDS,* COMMUNICATION IS ABOUT EXPRESSING A COMBINATION OF FACTS, FEELINGS, DRAMA, HUMOR AND CREATIVE IDEAS.

Now that we've reviewed all four styles, most of us can rank them in order from the style most like us to the one least like us. That's your unique blend.

What about those of you who identify with all four styles and can't place them in order of dominance? You probably have what's sometimes called the "facilitator" style, meaning that you are a fairly even blend of all styles. This gives you a lot of versatility and you are comfortable using all four styles. However, you are more likely than other styles to feel uncomfortable and even have conflict when others are communicating strongly in one dominant style to the exclusion of others.

Remember, we all can communicate in all four styles and do some of the time, but most of us have tendencies toward one or another style.

It's key to our success with others to understand how we come across so we can use style to gain receptivity to our message.

> MOST OF US HAVE TENDENCIES TOWARD CERTAIN STYLES. IT'S KEY TO OUR SUCCESS TO UNDERSTAND HOW WE COME ACROSS TO OTHERS SO WE CAN USE STYLE TO GAIN RECEPTIVITY TO OUR MESSAGE.

# SIGNALS OF OUR 4 COLOR STYLES

**"Prudent Planning Requires Patience, Precision and Preparation."**

| Planner | Precise | Patient |
|---------|---------|---------|
| Prudent | Probe | Prepared |
| Prove | Pattern | Predictability |
| Practice | Prioritize | Past Focused |
| Pace | Programs | Probabilities |
| Place | Projections | Prefers Logic |

## GREEN

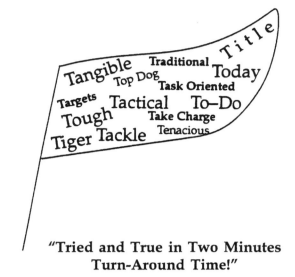

**"Tried and True in Two Minutes Turn-Around Time!"**

## BROWN

**"Let Me Lighten Your Load."**

## BLUE

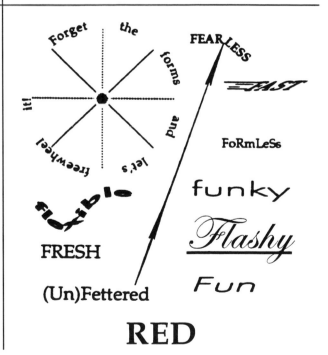

## RED

*Which color styles are you most comfortable using most often?*
*Which are you least comfortable with?*

# Style Descriptions

The following table provides a general description of the four styles. Remember: These are not mutually-exclusive descriptions. Some individuals may have a strong orientation to one style, while many people reflect a mixture of two or more styles depending upon the situation and the people involved.

| Green Style: | Brown Style: |
|---|---|
| When communicating in this style the person is logical, sequential and detail oriented. They often give historical data and discuss process. They tend to communicate literally and factually. They often understate emotions and appear reserved. They need time to process information and will not be rushed to make important decisions. They are skeptical of ideas that have not been evaluated. They like advance materials and accurate, thorough presentations. | When communicating in this style, the person is direct and brief. They focus on tasks and results. They are assertive and often speak in commands. They tend to want "yes" or "no," black or white answers. They don't want a lot of detail. They want to stay on point and discuss the "bottom line." They often do more than one thing at once and will appear impatient if things are moving too slowly. They like structured presentations. |
| **Blue Style:** | **Red Style:** |
| When communicating in this style the person often asks how others will be affected and whether they are being included in the decision-making process. They like to chat and form a personal connection before getting on task or discussing the business at hand. They often emote and present things in terms of feelings. They tend to clam up if they sense hostility or rudeness from others. They like people-oriented presentations. | When communicating in this style the person is often flamboyant, dramatic and energetic. They often tell jokes or stories. They like testimonials and creative examples. They tend to over-generalize for effect. They are bored by monotone, highly technical presentations. They often stray from the point of the meeting and are non-sequential presenters. They like humor, creative ideas, options and upbeat, fast-paced presentations. |

# TEST YOUR KNOWLEDGE

*Following are phrases from popular songs, common sayings and famous quotes. Beside each one, circle the color that might send such a signal:*

| | | | | |
|---|---|---|---|---|
| A. "Don't be cruel to a heart that's true." | Blue | Brown | Green | Red |
| B. "A stitch in time saves nine." | Blue | Brown | Green | Red |
| C. "Hit the road, Jack." | Blue | Brown | Green | Red |
| D. "I left my heart in San Francisco." | Blue | Brown | Green | Red |
| E. "I did it my way." | Blue | Brown | Green | Red |
| F. "Look before you leap." | Blue | Brown | Green | Red |
| G. "I'm so excited." | Blue | Brown | Green | Red |
| H. "Fifty ways to leave your lover." | Blue | Brown | Green | Red |
| I. "Don't mess with Texas!" | Blue | Brown | Green | Red |
| J. "Light my fire." | Blue | Brown | Green | Red |
| K. "People who need people." | Blue | Brown | Green | Red |
| L. "Let me ride…under sunny skies above/don't fence me in." | Blue | Brown | Green | Red |

ANSWERS ON PAGE 108

# NOTES

# 3

# Sophisticated Signals — Color Blends

I f the descriptions from chapter 2 seem somewhat one-dimensional, it is because none of us is pure. Now, this is not a comment on your ethics or morals. It means that no person communicates purely in one color. We send out much more complex communication signals than that.

Indeed, we access all four styles to one degree or another. Even if you think you are completely disorganized and disinterested in logic or detail — chances are you *do* have some Green in your style and you *can* send Green signals, if you choose.

However, there are usually two — or sometimes three — of the four "colors" that are easier for you to use in your day-to-day communication. Your dominant style — or your preferred "color blend" — is what *this* chapter is all about.

Look at the two cards that you placed on top when you did the color sort in chapter 2. This will tend to be your dominant color blend and will play a major role in the signals that you send. Let's take a look at the six color blend combinations and the signals associated with each of them.

> *"A moment's insight is sometimes worth a life's experience."*
>
> *- Oliver Wendell Holmes*

## BROWN-GREEN/GREEN-BROWN

Did you place the Brown and Green cards together (in either order) on top when you sorted your colors? This is the Brown/Green blend.

The *Green-Brown/Brown-Green* says: "I am prepared and get the job done. You can count on my decisions to be based on fact, logic and careful analysis."

The *Green-Brown/Brown-Greens* send signals that they are:

- Thoughtful decision makers;
- Planners who take timely action;
- Swayed by logic rather than emotion;
- Steady and goal oriented.

To persuade a *Green-Brown/Brown-Green*, don't emote. Be factual, logical, systematic and to the point.

## BROWN-RED/RED-BROWN

Did you place these two cards on top (in either order)?

The *Brown-Red/Red-Brown* blend says:

"Let's move! Let's move! And think outside of the box while you're moving…get smart, take chances. Keep your eyes on the prize."

Brown-Red/Red-Brown communicators send signals that they are:

- Creative decision makers;
- Flamboyant and yet results oriented;
- Impatient to do it *now*;
- Often entrepreneurial (risk takers and achievers).

So to persuade a *Brown-Red/Red-Brown*, be quick, refer to how they will benefit, use humor and testimonials.

TO PERSUADE A *GREEN-BROWN/ BROWN-GREEN*, DON'T EMOTE.

TO PERSUADE A *BROWN-RED/RED-BROWN* BE QUICK, SAY HOW THEY'LL BENEFIT AND USE HUMOR AND TESTIMONIALS.

## RED-BLUE/BLUE-RED:

If you put these two on top in your color sort, you send highly social communication signals.

The *Red-Blue/Blue-Red* blend says:

"I care about you as a person. I want to connect with you. And it's going to be fun! I'll inspire you. I'll make you laugh. You're gonna *love* hanging out with me."

The Red-Blue/Blue-Red communicators send signals that they are:

- Very expressive and emotive;
- Caring and fun;
- Inspirational;
- Flamboyant yet sensitive.

So to persuade a *Red-Blue/Blue-Red,* show compassion, reveal your feelings, be social (go to lunch) and have fun.

> TO PERSUADE A *RED-BLUE/BLUE-RED* SHOW COMPASSION, REVEAL YOUR FEELINGS, BE SOCIAL (GO TO LUNCH) AND HAVE FUN.

## BLUE-GREEN/GREEN-BLUE:

If you put these two cards on top, you send thoughtful, caring signals. Proportionately higher numbers of people in the helping professions put these cards on top: teachers, social workers, clinical psychologists, nurses and human resource professionals.

It makes sense when you think about it. People with this style blend tend to send signals that they are concerned both about people *and* about quality.

Blue-Green/Green-Blue communicators also tend to be the slowest decision-makers. They are especially concerned about decisions that are based on facts and that are supported by the people who will be affected by them. That's a lot to think about when you're trying to decide.

The *Blue-Green/Green-Blue* style says:

"I care about you and want to connect with you. Together, we can explore so many new ideas. We can share information. We can have a dialogue."

Blue-Green/Green-Blue communicators tend to send signals that they are:

- Caring and thoughtful;
- Concerned with producing a high quality result that has included the input of those affected;
- Comfortable both with intuition and analysis, logic and emotion.

To persuade a *Blue-Green/Green-Blue,* show compassion and stress your desire for a quality result.

> TO PERSUADE A *BLUE-GREEN/ GREEN-BLUE* CONNECT WITH THEM, PROVIDE INFORMATION ON HOW OTHERS WILL BE AFFECTED AND GIVE THEM TIME TO MAKE THEIR DECISION.

The four blends described above represent the *majority* color blends in North America. Some studies indicate that each blend represents approximately 22 percent of the total. That leaves about 12 percent of the population unaccounted for.

Following are the two blends that each comprise approximately 6-7 percent of the population.

## BLUE-BROWN/BROWN-BLUE:

We call this the "Mother Teresa" style as this world citizen embodied the results and relationship-oriented signals that this blend sends to others:

- Caring yet ready to press ahead;
- Wanting to include others in decision making while wanting to make the decision *quickly*;
- People oriented *and* task oriented.

The illustrative story here is of Mother Teresa and the bush pilot.

The bush pilot has flown a plane load of supplies into a remote jungle location. When the pilot lands, Mother Teresa comes out personally to greet him. She hugs him and thanks him for taking on this difficult mission. For five minutes, she engages him in a personal conversation asking the pilot where he's from, does he have any pictures of his family and how does he feel about doing this kind of work?

Then she quickly shifts gears. "We're going to need a lot more supplies. What I want you to do is get something to eat, rest and then get back here within 24 hours."

This story illustrates the mixed signals that a Blue-Brown/Brown-Blue communicator can send. That makes it really important for *Blue-Brown/Brown-Blues* to communicate which part of the blend is dominant in a given situation. ("Honey, I love you but right now I'm task focused so please just take the garbage out.")

So to persuade a *Blue-Brown/Brown-Blue,* be friendly and get to the point.

## GREEN-RED/RED-GREEN

This is an unusual blend that can be stunningly successful or confusing to the listener. Green-Red/Red-Green communicators can sometimes move back and forth between their Green (plan, be logical, get details) and their Red (be spontaneous, intuitive, the heck with details!) and leave others thinking that they are "waffling."

Like the *Blue-Brown/Brown-Blue,* it becomes very important for the *Green-Red/Red-Green* to signal just *which* part is dominant in a given situation. ("I know I asked you to work out a detailed plan but, right now, I'm in my spontaneous mode, so just tell me the most fascinating thing in that plan.") Sending clear signals about your dominant style can avoid confusion, frustration and a lot of unfair judgments of you.

So to persuade a *Green-Red/Red-Green,* be versatile. Show some flair and a full grasp of the details.

> TO PERSUADE A *BLUE-BROWN/ BROWN-BLUE,* BE FRIENDLY AND GET TO THE POINT.
>
> TO PERSUADE *GREEN-RED/RED-GREEN,* BE VERSATILE. SHOW SOME FLAIR AND A FULL GRASP OF THE DETAILS.

# COLOR STYLE TENDENCIES

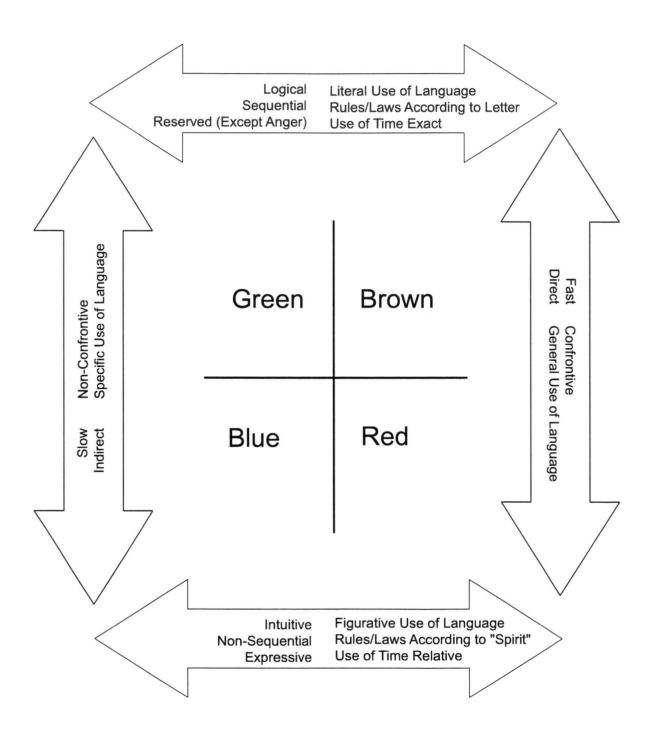

Logical
Sequential
Reserved (Except Anger)

Literal Use of Language
Rules/Laws According to Letter
Use of Time Exact

Non-Confrontive
Specific Use of Language

Slow
Indirect

Fast
Direct

Confrontive
General Use of Language

Green    Brown

Blue    Red

Intuitive
Non-Sequential
Expressive

Figurative Use of Language
Rules/Laws According to "Spirit"
Use of Time Relative

*Where do you fit on this axis?*

# Success Signals Profile

To learn more about your preferred color blend, please complete the profile on the next page.

The profile will give you even more detail about your unique style of communication and can help you understand more fully the signals you send.

In each of the four columns, check off the words or phrases that are *really like you*. For example, if you think you are really "flamboyant," check that word. (On the other hand, if you are only flamboyant on Halloween and only then when you are wearing a full mask, don't check it.)

Complete your profile now. Don't take more than five minutes to do this. If you take too long, you will tend to "over-think."

> THE PROFILE WILL GIVE YOU EVEN MORE DETAIL ABOUT YOUR UNIQUE STYLE OF COMMUNICATION.

# Success Signals Profile

**INSTRUCTIONS:** Place a check by each word that is **really** like you. If the meaning of the word is unclear, do not place a check by it. Additional profiles are included in the Appendix.

| | | | |
|---|---|---|---|
| ____ accountable (w) | ____ driver (w) | ____ likes change (x) | ____ responsible (w) |
| ____ accuracy (z) | ____ dutiful (w) | ____ link together (y) | ____ results oriented (w) |
| ____ achievement (w) | ____ efficient (w) | ____ listening (y) | ____ risk taker (x) |
| ____ adventurer (x) | ____ emotional (y) | ____ literal (z) | ____ romantic (y) |
| ____ agreeable (y) | ____ enthusiastic (x) | ____ logical (z) | ____ saving (w) |
| ____ amiable (y) | ____ exacting (z) | ____ loving (y) | ____ sensitive (y) |
| ____ analytical (z) | ____ excitable (x) | ____ loyal (y) | ____ sentimental (y) |
| ____ asks (y) | ____ exciting (x) | ____ mastery (z) | ____ serious (z) |
| ____ authority (w) | ____ fast (x) | ____ mover (x) | ____ skeptical (z) |
| ____ avoids conflict (y) | ____ feelings first (y) | ____ orderly (z) | ____ spends (x) |
| ____ being accepted (y) | ____ flamboyant (x) | ____ organized (z) | ____ spontaneous (x) |
| ____ being in control (w) | ____ flashy (x) | ____ originality (x) | ____ spurt worker (x) |
| ____ bottom line (w) | ____ flexible (x) | ____ patient (z) | ____ status (w) |
| ____ budgets (z) | ____ freedom (x) | ____ people centered (y) | ____ stimulating (x) |
| ____ careful (z) | ____ friendly (y) | ____ perfectionist (z) | ____ strategist (z) |
| ____ cautious action (z) | ____ fun (x) | ____ performer (x) | ____ strong-willed (w) |
| ____ challenge authority (x) | ____ future focus (x) | ____ planner (z) | ____ structure (w) |
| ____ conceptual (z) | ____ gestures (x) | ____ playful (x) | ____ supportive (y) |
| ____ conforming (y) | ____ giving (y) | ____ powerful (w) | ____ sympathetic (y) |
| ____ considerate (y) | ____ harmonious (y) | ____ practical (w) | ____ take charge (w) |
| ____ creative (x) | ____ helps others (y) | ____ precise (z) | ____ team oriented (y) |
| ____ decisive (w) | ____ history (z) | ____ predicts (z) | ____ tells (w) |
| ____ demanding (w) | ____ honest feelings (y) | ____ prepared (w) | ____ theoretical (z) |
| ____ dependable (y) | ____ impatient (w) | ____ present focused (y) | ____ thinker (z) |
| ____ detail oriented (z) | ____ implementer (w) | ____ prioritizes (z) | ____ tough (w) |
| ____ direct (w) | ____ impulsive (x) | ____ probing (z) | ____ traditional (w) |
| ____ discipline (w) | ____ innovative (z) | ____ quality (z) | ____ warmth (y) |
| ____ do it now (w) | ____ law & order (w) | ____ questioning (z) | ____ willing (y) |
| ____ down with routine (x) | ____ leader (w) | ____ rapid reaction (x) | ____ works best alone (z) |
| ____ dramatic (x) | ____ lighthearted (x) | ____ relater (y) | ____ zestful (x) |

# Turn the page for information on how to interpret your profile.

The following are instructions for how to interpret your profile.

1. Each word has a letter "w," "x," "y" or "z" next to it. Add up how many words with a "w" next to them that you checked. Then add up the "x," "y" and "z" words. Record them below.

___ "w" words
___ "x" words
___ "y" words
___ "z" words

"w" = Brown style signals
"x" = Red style signals
"y" = Blue style signals
"z" = Green style signals

> IF YOU HAVE 20 OR MORE CHECKS IN A STYLE, YOU ARE PROBABLY VERY COMFORTABLE SENDING SIGNALS IN THIS STYLE.

2. If you have 20 or more checks next to a particular style (Red, Brown, Blue, Green), you are very comfortable sending signals in this style. It is probably a dominant style for you. Please note that you may have more than 20 checks in two, three *or* four columns. More about that later.

3. *If you have fewer than five checks* next to a particular style (Red, Brown, Blue, Green), you are *not* very comfortable sending signals in this style. You still have the style *available* to you but it takes more energy for you to "bring the style up" and use it effectively.

4. *If you have similar numbers* next to two styles, you may be a true blend. That means you are a balanced combination of both styles and your communication signals will be a mix of the two styles.

5. *If you have similar numbers* next to three styles, we call this a tripartite style. Here you are a balanced combination of three styles.

6. *If you have similar numbers in all four styles:* You have the "facilitator style." You send balanced, blended signals to others; people don't experience you as dominant in one or two styles. You move easily from one style to another, depending on the situation and the needs of your listeners.

What if your profile is very different from the way you sorted your cards? We generally suggest that you rely more heavily on the card sort since it gives you three sets of signals to assist you — words, graphics and colors — whereas the profile gives you only words. However, there may be other reasons for a difference between your profile and your card order. For example: when numbers are close together, card order may be different. This is not significant since the proximity of the numbers is indicating a two, three or four "blend" of colors as the dominant style. When there are major discrepancies between card order and numbers, this may be due to fatigue, illness, stress or the occurrence of a significant change (new job, marriage, divorce, new baby, etc.) that often skews self-perception. You may want to wait a month and repeat the Success Signals Profile over a period of two-six months. There are extra profiles at the end of the book.

> IF YOU HAVE SIMILAR NUMBERS IN ALL FOUR STYLES, YOU SEND BALANCED, BLENDED SIGNALS.

# NOTES

# 4

# Getting Our Signals Crossed — Styles Opposites

**D**id you ever meet someone for the first time and feel like you'd known him or her your whole life? Your styles mesh and you understand each other perfectly. You walk away smiling.

Unfortunately, we've all had the other kind of experience. We meet someone — or interact with someone we've known for a long time — and we feel like we're "talking to a brick wall!" We leave the encounter frustrated. Maybe we even have a fight before we go.

> *"To speak of 'mere' words is much like speaking of 'mere dynamite.'"*
>
> -C. J. Ducasse

## WHEN STYLE LEADS TO CONFLICT

There are four main types of differences that result in human conflict. We call these the "VIPS," differences in:

- Values;
- Interests;
- Perceptions;
- Styles.

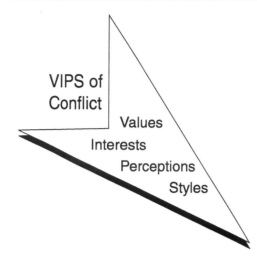

**VIPS of Conflict**

Values
Interests
Perceptions
Styles

This book is focused mainly on the conflicts arising from differences in *style*[1] but let's take a minute to review all four sources of conflict.

## VALUE DIFFERENCES:

When we have fundamental differences in what we believe to be of core importance in our lives, we can end up in conflict with those who are different from us. For example, the pro-choice/pro-life debate in the United States stems from differences in values and associated beliefs. The bad news is that conflicts that come from value differences are usually the toughest to resolve. The good news is that value differences are usually responsible for less than 10 percent of all human conflict.

## INTEREST DIFFERENCES:

When your needs and my needs in a given situation are different, we can end up in conflict. For example, when a company needs to cut costs, the company management may be interested in finding the areas of largest cost savings while employees may be more interested in saving jobs during the cost cutting time. These differences, although far from irreconcilable, often lead to strife.

## PERCEPTION DIFFERENCES:

You and I may look at the same situation and interpret it differently. We view the world from our own set of assumptions. If we do not question these assumptions, we believe that the way that *we* see things is "the right way." That means that *your* way (if it's different)

---

[1] *To get more information on how to deal with differences involving values, interests and perceptions contact Agreement Dynamics at 206-546-8048 or email us at hq@agreementdynamics.com.*

must be "the wrong way." Two parents see that Johnny is not doing well in school. Dad—who assumes that socializing gets in the way of schoolwork—perceives that Johnny's spending too much time hanging out with his friends or talking on the phone. Mom—who believes that Johnny is not motivated by the way the curriculum is taught—perceives that the teacher's approach is the problem. Now both may have a piece of the puzzle but they may spend more time fighting about who's "right" than solving the problem.

## STYLE DIFFERENCES:

Somewhere in the neighborhood of 70 percent of all human conflict is caused by differences in *style*. Remember style isn't "what" we're trying to get across, but "how." The difference here is in the *communication signals that we send*. We figuratively "get our signals crossed."

There are three causes of style-based conflicts:
1. Message mistranslation
2. Style stereotyping
3. Styles in stress[2]

MESSAGE MISTRANSLATION

A dominant Blue style communicator asks a dominant Brown style communicator for an impromptu meeting late in the work day. The Brown agrees, but frequently checks her watch. The Blue assumes the Brown is uninterested in what she has to say and just wants to get rid of her. The Brown is worried about getting to her daughter's day care before it closes. Both start feeling tense and assume the other is being inconsiderate.

> MOST HUMAN CONFLICT IS CAUSED BY DIFFERENCES IN STYLE.

---

[2] *For information on style stereotyping and styles in stress, see chapters 7 and 8.*

Why does this happen? It happens because mistranslation and misunderstanding usually occurs when mesages are sent in one style and received in another.

In other words, you are most likely to have a style-based conflict with your style opposite. Looking at the order of your color cards, your style opposite is someone whose dominant style is the color style you have ranked last in your color card order.

You can learn to avert—or at least defuse—these style-based conflicts if you understand their causes.

### The Brown/Green Conflict

If you send very strong Brown signals but are "weak" in the Green, you are most likely to have a style-based conflict with someone who sends strong Green signals. This style-based conflict often revolves around how time is used and different approaches to decision making.

High Brown (low Green) communicators think that Green communicators just take too long to decide anything and that they get mired down in endless process. This creates a lot of stress for the high *Brown* who is afraid that opportunities will be lost and other things will get needlessly delayed.

High Green (low Brown) communicators regard the Brown communicators as *reckless* because from the *Green's* vantage point, *Browns* make decisions without all the facts and without careful analysis of the relevant information.

Picture, if you will, a law firm with one dominant *Brown* and one dominant *Green* partner. The *Brown* partner is ready to call it quits. "My partner is anal-retentive!" she says in frustration.

The *Green* partner is equally frustrated. "My partner's going to ruin this firm with her "shoot-from-the-hip" approach. Do you know how many *problems*

> GREEN-BROWN STYLE-BASED CONFLICTS OFTEN REVOLVE AROUND HOW TIME IS USED AND DIFFERENT APPROACHES TO DECISION MAKING.

we've had because she has got to make an instant decision?"

But what if each partner saw the other's decision-making style as an asset rather than a liability? When choosing a new associate for the firm, the *Brown* partner could rely on her *Green* counterpart to put the candidates through a rigorous process, one that the *Brown* partner would have no patience for. On the other hand, the *Green* partner could rely on his *Brown* counterpart to make those "think-on-your-feet" judgment calls that courtroom situations sometimes require.

It's not a matter of "good" or "bad" decision-making. It's *appropriate* decision making that creates success.

### THE BROWN/RED CONFLICT

Communicators, who are high on the Brown side and low on the Red, value structure. After all, if you have all the rules spelled out, there's less confusion and you can get the task done faster. High *Reds* — with their spirit of freedom and impatience with rules — can make the structure-loving Brown communicator want to climb the walls.

I was once called in to mediate a dispute between a dominant *Brown* and a dominant *Red*. The *Red* began his statement of the issue by attacking the *Brown* as a "control freak." Not to be outdone, the *Brown* shot back, "Well, at least I'm not a deviant like you who has no respect for anything."

But the issue is not, when you think about it, freedom versus structure. The key to success is knowing when, where and how much structure is useful and when, where and how much freedom is useful. I have a friend whose husband is a *High Brown (low Red)*. Her teenage daughter, on the other hand, is...you guessed it... *High Red (low Brown)*.

They used to argue — not over *whether* to do homework — but *where!* You see, the daughter liked to do homework all over the house. One of her favorite spots

> RED-BROWN
> STYLE-BASED
> CONFLICTS OFTEN
> REVOLVE
> AROUND
> FREEDOM VERSUS
> STRUCTURE.

was her bedroom floor. On school nights, the floor was strewn with textbooks, papers and the teenager's laptop. There, amidst apparent chaos, the girl worked away, usually to music pounding from her stereo. "Why did we bother to buy that girl a desk?" Dad would say in frustration. "You're supposed to do your homework at a *desk!*"

For Dad, the structure of working at a desk seemed important. To the teenage daughter, it seemed an unbearable burden to be so hemmed in.

Finally, Dad realized that there are issues where structure is important and others where freedom is important. So, my friend and her husband put certain rules into place: 1) you must finish homework before you can use the phone; and 2) music must be played softly. This structure helped the teenage daughter. And she remained free to hang upside down while she worked.

### THE RED/BLUE CONFLICT

This conflict is about the nature of commitment in a relationship. Basically, when a dominant *Blue* is in a relationship, commitment means *keeping in touch*, calling just to "chat." A flaming *Red* (without much Blue) has no such need. To them, commitment is expressed differently. *Reds* are neither creatures of routine, nor is time a linear continuum for them. For example, two *Reds* can be great friends and never even talk to each other for weeks or months at a time. Then one day one of them calls the other and they pick up their conversation like it was yesterday. This, of course, works fine with other *Reds*. But with *Blues*, it's important for others to be more regular in their contact and to periodically express how much they value the relationship.

It's equally important for *Blues* to cut their *Red* friends and family some slack—to recognize that *Reds* usually

> RED-BLUE STYLE-BASED CONFLICTS ARE ABOUT THE NATURE OF COMMITMENT IN A RELATIONSHIP.

have too many balls in the air, are naturally disorganized and often just don't think to call even though they really do care.

### The Blue/Green Conflict

This one is about people versus process, particularly in decision-making situations. If you are a high Green communicator who has little Blue in your style, then you believe that—if proper procedures are followed—most people should be okay with the decision. On the other hand, if you are *high Blue (low Green),* you are likely to say, "Procedures mean little if the people weren't involved with the decision making."

Imagine two supervisors having a hallway conversation:

*High Green:* "How's the new computer system working in your Section?"

*High Blue:* "Nothing's working right now."

*High Green:* "What do you mean?"

*High Blue:* "The staff really feels burned that nobody asked them what they thought."

*High Green* (a little annoyed and amazed): "But, we had a *process* to select the computer system. We formed a *task force.* A representative from your section could have volunteered. And we reviewed all of the options on the market. We eliminated the ones that did not meet our criteria..."

*High Blue:* "With all your process, was it too much to ask that someone talk to the human beings who use those computers?"

*High Green:* "Well, we can't talk to everyone, that's why we developed a process. It's unreasonable to expect us to hold everybody's hand whenever we make a change around here."

*High Blue:* "What's unreasonable is how insensitive this company is to its employees..."

> BLUE-GREEN STYLE-BASED CONFLICTS ARE USUALLY ABOUT PEOPLE VERSUS PROCESS, PARTICULARLY IN DECISION-MAKING.

Well, you get the picture.

Of course, what we want to tell these two supervisors is, "It's not people *or* process. It's people *and* process that makes for good decisions. Each of you has a piece of the solution. Maybe, if you had worked together and acknowledged the legitimacy of each other's approach..."

THE BLUE/BROWN CONFLICT

If the *Blue/Green* conflict is about people versus process, you can probably guess that the *Blue/Brown* conflict is about people versus results. Let's join Bob *Brown* Jones and Betty *Blue* Jones, talking in their kitchen about their son's poor grades.

"That's it!" says Bob *Brown*. "That kid will have no life until his grades come up. No friends, no sleepovers, no extracurricular activities..."

"Now, honey," answers Betty *Blue*, "We can't stop him from having friends. And extracurricular activities make him a well-rounded person."

"Round, my foot!" retorts Bob. "His grades are round, all right. Big fat ZEROS. Well, the party's over. It's our job to help him get *results*. And I'd appreciate your support in this. I don't want to be the bad guy, as usual."

"Now, Bob," Betty says, with a patient sigh. "Developing social skills is essential to his success in life."

"Oh yeah," retorts Bob, "Well it's never been a problem for me. I was raised to keep my nose to the grindstone."

"Well, it may not be a problem for you, but what about the rest of us who have to live with you?" Betty replies.

...And the conversation goes downhill from there.

Of course, Betty and Bob both have something important to contribute to their son's success. It's not people versus results. It's people *and* results.

> BLUE-BROWN STYLE-BASED CONFLICTS ARE USUALLY ABOUT PEOPLE VERSUS RESULTS.

This conflict is about the use of language. Remember that Red-style communicators love to exaggerate, use hyperbole, tell stories and give testimonials to illustrate their points. Green-style communicators, on the other hand, want to hear facts, data and logic. To them, all of this exaggeration renders the speaker less than credible. So, a high Red (low Green) speaker will drive a high Green (low Red) speaker to the edge of distraction. And vice versa, of course.

Here's Steve, a Red teen with little Green in his style, talking to his older sister. "Oh, man, you won't believe this! Yesterday, I went over to Greg's house. It was the greatest party in the history of the world. There were millions of people there and they all knew me. It was so cool. Everywhere I went they were yelling, 'Hey Steve.' 'Hey Steve.' I mean it was like I was a celebrity or something."

"Now Steve," says his Green sister. "In the history of the world there have to have been other parties that were at least as good as this one. And there couldn't' have been millions of people there, especially since Greg's house can't be more than 2,500 square feet."

As Steve chases his big sister up the stairs, we can see that this argument is all about literal versus figurative use of language.

> RED-GREEN CONFLICT IS ABOUT USE OF LANGUAGE.

# CONCLUSION

You are most likely to have a style conflict caused by mistranslation with someone who has a strong style preference that is very different from yours. Look at your last card and think about it. Do any of the conflicts described above seem familiar to you?

Part of dispelling these types of conflicts is to understand them. Once you do, you are in a much better position to see a way out of them.

In our next chapter, we'll look at how to prevent or defuse conflicts between different styles.

# NOTES

# 5

# Keeping Opposites on Track

Style opposites are often attracted to each other (at first). Many of you are married to your style opposite (or you were!). When people who have very different style preferences irritate or antagonize each other, it's usually because they misunderstand "what" is being communicated. "How" one person communicates is so different that the message is mistranslated.

> "Where all think alike, no one thinks very much."
>
> – Walter Lippman

Here's a typical workplace example:

*Blue* knocks on the door.

*Brown*: "Come in."

*Blue:* "Have you got a minute, Joe, because we've got a problem?"

*Brown:* "What is it?"

*Blue* sits down, then looks up with a pained expression: "Our overtime is going through the roof. I think it's because morale is so low. I mean, people are seriously depressed. Nobody even wants to come to work much less do what it takes to get done on time."

*Brown:* "What do you want me to do about it?"

*Blue:* "If you could just understand what we're all going through. I mean everyone has been working like dogs for the last six months with no pats on the back. We all feel like no one cares. It's just so hard—I mean are you feeling my pain?"

*Brown:* "What do you think this is, Gladys, a therapy session? I mean, this is a job, J-O-B, job. You ought to know that. You're a supervisor. You're paid to work here, and if you and everybody else around here can't get it together, I'll find someone who can. Now buck up! We've all got problems. Just don't bring them to work!"

*Blue* leaves without saying anything, muttering under her breath with her back to the boss: "We'll see who leaves around here!"

- Imagine you were the Blue style communicator in this example. What could you have done differently to avoid this conflict and to maximize receptivity to your message?
- Now imagine you were the Brown style communicator in this example. What could you have done differently to avoid this conflict and to maximize receptivity to your message?

Either the *Blue* or the *Brown* could prevent this communication and relationship breakdown by:

1. "Acknowledging" the other person's interests and concerns. (This is not the same as agreeing with what the other person has said.)
2. Using the other person's style—or at least acknowledging it to state what they want. For example, in the case of the Blue communicator, not emoting, staying on task and by making recommendations to solve the problem.

In fact, let's look at how the *Blue*, who initiated the conversation, could have approached her boss in a way that got his cooperation.

*Blue* knocks on the door.

*Brown:* "Come in."

*Blue:* "Have you got a minute, Joe, because we've got a problem."

*Brown:* "What is it?"

*Blue:* "Our overtime is going through the roof. I've got a couple ideas on how to fix it. Is this a good time to run them by you?"

*Brown:* "Yeah, okay."

*Blue:* "Because we've been understaffed for the last six months during our busy season, people are getting burned out and morale has taken a nose dive. It's affecting productivity. There are two things that will turn this around. One I can do, but the other has to come from you."

*Brown:* "What do you mean?"

*Blue:* "First, I've stepped up the hiring and training process and I can let the employees know that we'll be fully staffed in another two months. In the meantime, you've got to help me give them some pats on the back."

*Brown:* "Oh no, you know I hate that touchy-feely crap!"

*Blue:* "I know, Joe, and I'm not asking you to be touchy-feely. That's what you've got me for, right?"

*Brown* (kind of laughs): "Right."

*Blue:* "You're the Department Director and people respect you, Joe. They need to know that you respect them and the extra effort they've put out. I only need a few minutes of your time at the next staff meeting."

*Brown:* "What do you want me to do?"

> TO OVERCOME COMMUNICATION DIFFICULTIES ENCOUNTERED WITH YOUR STYLE OPPOSITE, FIRST ACKNOWLEDGE THE OTHER PERSON'S INTERESTS AND CONCERNS.

*Blue:* "I'll send you a memo spelling it out, but basically, I want you to give them a pep talk and express your appreciation for their hard work (if you can be sincere about it)."

*Brown:* "Of course I can be sincere. I may be a hardass, but that doesn't mean I don't care about our employees. They're one hell of a crew! Second to none."

*Blue:* "That's exactly what I want you to say."

*Brown:* "That's it? Okay, you got it!"

**What a difference your style makes! How about at home? Let's look in on a *Green* and a *Red* couple who are discussing their upcoming vacation.**

*Green:* "I've been thinking about our vacation to Europe and I got some information on sights we might want to see. We'll need to sign up soon because some of these are only accessible by tours that get booked in advance. What do you think?"

*Red:* "Hey, I think it's a vacation, not boot camp! I want to do whatever I feel like when I get there."

*Green:* "That's fine, but if we don't plan ahead and make some choices now we'll miss out on a lot of things. I mean, why go to Europe if you just want to hang out? Go lie on a beach somewhere, if that's what you want."

*Red:* "Well maybe I will if that's what it takes to have a real vacation. Let's be spontaneous—check out what's available when we get there and then choose. So we miss a few things, big deal!"

*Green:* "It is a big deal. We've been saving and planning for this vacation for a long time......"

*Red* interrupts: "You mean you've been planning. I'm sure you've got a computerized itinerary all ready to go."

> TO OVERCOME THE COMMUNICATION DIFFICULTIES ENCOUNTERED WITH YOUR STYLE OPPOSITE, USE OR ACKNOWLEDGE THE OTHER PERSON'S STYLE.

*Green:* "Well if someone around here didn't plan and save (I might add), we'd never do anything."

*Red:* "What's that supposed to mean? Are you going to start lecturing me about money again?"

*Green* throws up hands and says: "We'll discuss this when you're willing to be rational."

*Green* walks away. As *Green* is leaving, *Red* yells out: "The hell we will—we'll discuss it now. Hey! Why do you always walk away when I try to explain my side of things?"

Exasperated, the *Red* kicks a chair and walks out.

- Imagine you were the *Green* style communicator in this example. What could you have done differently to avoid this conflict and to maximize receptivity to your message?
- Now imagine you were the *Red* style communicator in this example. What could you have done differently to avoid this conflict and to maximize receptivity to your message?

> WHAT A DIFFERENCE STYLE MAKES IN CONFLICT RESOLUTION.

Again, either party could very likely have prevented this argument by:

1. Acknowledging what the other person wants;
2. Using the other person's style—or at least acknowledging it to state what they want.

Since the *Green* spouse initiated the conversation, let's see how he or she could have communicated to maximize the *Red* partner's receptivity to the *Green's* concerns.

*Green:* "I've been thinking about our vacation to Europe and I've got some information on sites we might want to see. We'll need to sign up soon because some of these are only accessible by tours that get booked in advance. What do you think?"

*Red:* "Hey, I think it's a vacation, not boot camp! I want to do whatever I feel like when I get there."

*Green:* "Okay sweetheart. I think I'm hearing you. You want to have maximum flexibility to do what you want in the moment. Is that right?"

*Red:* "You got it! I want to go with the flow. Sometimes chill out, sometimes sight see. Take it as it comes."

*Green:* "Okay, I'm willing to loosen up a little, but you know me, I need to have some things figured out. I can relax, have fun and even be spontaneous if I do some advance planning."

*Red:* "I know, you're the master of "planned spontaneity."

*Green* laughs: "You're right. I could get pretty wild with a map and a palm pilot. Seriously, though, there are a few things I don't want to miss. Should I just book myself on some tours and you can come if you want and there's space available, or would you like to choose a couple now that you don't want to miss?"

*Red:* "Well, I like both your ideas. How about I look at those brochures and maybe pick out one or two or however many things I really want to do and you can book them. Some things you want to see I may opt out. So how about it?"

*Green:* "Sounds good to me. I'd love to do some tours with you, but I don't mind leaving others open as to whether you decide to go or not."

*Red:* "Hey, all right. I think this is going to be a great vacation!"

Couple hugs.

Once again, unnecessary conflict was avoided because the signals sent were clear, respectful and acknowledged the other person's perspective.

# NOTES

# NOTES

# 6

# Sending Success Signals:
# How to Get Others to Listen

Imagine yourself in a room with someone who speaks only Italian. You happen to speak some Italian yourself but it is not your native language. You are a Portuguese-speaking person.

How do you communicate?

You have a choice. You can think to yourself, "Well, this guy will just have to accept me as I am—a Portuguese-speaking person," and you can speak Portuguese to him. He won't understand you but you will be speaking your native language.

Or you could speak Italian. You will both get a lot more about of the conversation that way, won't you?

Style and its associated signals is a language, too. Throughout this book, you have been learning the languages of style. This section gives you a few tips on putting your learning to use—and sending success signals to people of *all* styles. This will not only help minimize style conflicts caused by mistranslation, but it will dramatically increase others' receptivity to your message.

> *"Vive
> la
> difference!"*

# EARS WIDE OPEN

When you communicate with another person, you want them to be receptive to your messages. Approaching them at least some of the time in their own language is the key to whether they will *really* listen to you.

Remember that we have all of the four styles available to us in some measure. When you are not particularly comfortable using a certain "color," it may take more energy to access that style within you. However, you *can do it.* You will need to judge when it's worth the effort.

So what signals work best when dealing with a person speaking each "color" style?

## BROWN

Figure 6-1 gives you a list of tips for bringing up more of your Brown when dealing with someone speaking in a dominant Brown mode.

We can sum up this chart in one line:

GET TO THE POINT!

When approaching a person in dominant Brown mode, do not emote or hit them with lots of details. Start by talking about the bottom line—the problem you want to fix. If you are bringing a problem to a *Brown,* also bring your recommended solutions. If you don't, the task-oriented *Brown* might immediately jump in with his own solution.

WHEN COMMUNICATING WITH *BROWNS,* GET TO THE POINT!

## FIGURE 6-1: TIPS FOR COMMUNICATING BROWN

These are tips on how to bring up more of your Brown when dealing with someone in a dominant Brown mode:

### DO:

- Separate "business time" from "social time";
- Be direct, brief and to the point;
- Present relevant facts in a clear organized manner;
- Give an overview or outline first and then ask how much detail they want at this time;
- Keep discussions free of interruptions;
- Stay on task;
- Ask how much time they have for this meeting or discussion and finish by or before their allotted time frame;
- Present alternatives (rather than one way) to achieve desired results;
- Express disagreement in terms of information and facts rather than feelings or personalities.

### DON'T:

- Take offense if they do other things while meeting or talking with you;
- Challenge their views in front of others;
- Engage in chit-chat or socialize before getting down to business;
- Show up late, wander off task, waste time or request anything you won't want to accept;
- Exaggerate or make unrealistic commitments;
- Use feeling or relationship examples to persuade;
- Criticize them personally or attack their competency;
- Hug, embrace or pat them on the back unless they do so first;
- Appear disorganized or unsure of your objectives.

## GREEN

Figure 6-2 gives you a list of tips for bringing up more of your Green when dealing with someone speaking in a dominant Green mode.

Although Green-style communicators would find it hard to sum things up in one sentence (there are so many aspects of the chart to consider), we will sum it up:

DO YOUR HOMEWORK.

If someone is speaking Green, they will respond to facts, logic, reason and research. Do not approach them with "pie in the sky" ideas or heartfelt testimonials. Just make sure you know what you are talking about. If you have a problem, explain it in a calm, rational manner. You do not need to know all of the answers. You just need to show the *Green* that you have thought about things.

WHEN
COMMUNICATING
WITH *GREENS,*
BE PREPARED.

## FIGURE 6-2: TIPS FOR COMMUNICATING GREEN

These are tips on how to bring up more of your Green when dealing with someone in a dominant Green mode:

### DO:

- Come prepared with background information, historical data, references and other relevant data to support your presentation;
- Present information in a logical, sequential and thorough manner;
- Ask questions to gather more information about their needs and process preferences;
- Allow time for them to consider and verify your information;
- Explain the process or criteria you used to develop your views and the context in which you are presenting information;
- Be specific, precise and accurate;
- Be serious, cautious and careful in your demeanor;
- Acknowledge other viewpoints and communicate your willingness to analyze all potential options;
- Prepare advance materials and send them out before the meeting.

### DON'T:

- Fly by the seat of your pants or pretend to be an expert if you are not;
- Jump around, raise ideas "out of order," or give information in a "piecemeal" fashion;
- Assume you know what will interest them or how they prefer to process information;
- Make a commitment and then fail to deliver;
- Pressure them for a decision or rush through a presentation;
- Interpret their serious demeanor to mean they disapprove of you or are rejecting your views;
- Don't exaggerate, over-generalize or use flamboyant or trendy phrases;
- Tell them to "be bold" or "throw caution to the wind";
- Ask them to "trust" you;
- Use emotion or appeals to personal relationships to influence them.

BLUE

Figure 6-3 gives you a list of tips for bringing up more of your Blue when dealing with someone conversing in a dominant Blue mode.

To sum things up, BE SINCERE when approaching a person speaking *Blue*. Remember that Blue-style communicators are highly sensitive to subtle signals. They can spot a phony from a mile away, so do not use false flattery or cajoling. They will see right through it.

Instead, take a moment to MAKE A HUMAN CONNECTION. Let's say that you approach a *Blue* regarding a business issue and they say, "Oh, by the way, I heard that your wife had surgery. I hope she's better now." Take a moment to acknowledge the speaker's concern. "Thanks for asking. She's recovering nicely." You will find the level of reception to *your* message skyrockets when you communicate on a personal level with a *Blue*.

> WHEN COMMUNICATING WITH *BLUES,* BE SINCERE.

## FIGURE 6-3: TIPS FOR COMMUNICATING BLUE

These are tips on how to bring up more of your Blue when dealing with someone in a dominant Blue mode:

## DO:

- Make a personal connection and focus first on relationship building;
- Talk in terms of how your request will help people or improve relationships;
- Show that you have feelings;
- Ask them to share their ideas and feelings;
- Sincerely praise their efforts and input;
- Expect to work through problems and issues together;
- Periodically ask them if they are comfortable with how things are going and ask for their input before some key decisions are made;
- Make it safe for them to express their views;
- Show patience and build in time for putting them at ease and demonstrating that you value them as a person.

## DON'T:

- Act too busy to listen to their needs;
- Launch right into a business or work-related discussion before you've established social rapport;
- Talk only in terms of facts, process or innovation;
- Use false flattery or any form of manipulation;
- Use put-downs about being too "touchy-feely";
- Ask them to figure out a solution alone and come back to you with an answer;
- Personally attack them, argue or use commands;
- Make too many key decisions without consulting them and don't pressure them for quick answers;
- Come on too strong or make threats.

## RED

Figure 6-4 gives you tips for bringing up your Red.
One word: ENERGY!

Three words: DON'T BE BORING!

You get the picture. When approaching someone speaking Red, start with the most interesting, exciting and enjoyable aspect of your topic. "You have got to check out that *Success Signals* workshop! It rocks! I never saw so many people having fun and learning so much in no time flat!"

Also, give the Red communicator OPTIONS. People in the Red mode do not like to be told that they have no choices. With a sense of freedom, Red-style communicators will be much more receptive to your message.

---

WHEN
COMMUNICATING
WITH *REDS*,
DON'T BE BORING!

---

There are times even when you use the other person's style and acknowledge what they want but things still go haywire. Then what? Read on...

## FIGURE 6-4: TIPS FOR COMMUNICATING RED

These are tips on how to bring up more of your Red when dealing with someone in a dominant Red mode:

### DO:

- Present information with energy and excitement;
- Give them options along with the impact of each option;
- Be fast-paced, non-sequential and up-beat;
- Use humor, vivid examples and offer lots of ideas for taking action;
- Let them know your deadlines in a nonthreatening manner;
- Mix business and socializing;
- Use testimonials from well-known people and others they admire;
- Encourage their participation and even interruptions of your presentations;
- Let them know you're willing to experiment and try new things.

### DON'T:

- Read a document to them or use a lot of technical data to influence them;
- Tell them they have no alternatives;
- Order them to do anything;
- Use logic or "need for consistency" as reasons for accepting your point of view;
- Be too serious;
- Focus only on business;
- Structure meetings too much or tell them when they can participate;
- Tell them they must do something because it is "policy" or "house rules";
- Speak in a monotone or fail to make frequent eye contact.

# NOTES

# 7

# Appreciating All Styles:
# The True Signal of Success

Y ou've done everything this book has recommended and still the other person won't listen or be reasonable. In this case, style differences may not be the cause of the problem. But before making that judgment, check out two other possibilities.

> *"In matters of style, swim with the currents. In matters of principle, stand like a rock."*
>
> *– Thomas Jefferson*

## STYLE STEREOTYPING

The first is to see if there is—"style stereotyping." All of us go there sometimes. Any negative bias we have about a particular style may cause us to stereotype it in terms of extremes. Whenever we stereotype others, we also send signals (even if unintended) that we are better or that they are at fault. This quickly creates a negative reaction and conflict often results. Here are the common mistakes we make:

### STEREOTYPE: "BROWN-STYLE COMMUNICATORS ARE RIGID OR CONTROLLING."

We observe their tendency to talk in short sentences, state requests as orders and seek structure. If we do not relate to the Brown style, we can interpret this as uncaring or controlling.

This is because we misunderstand how *Browns* use language. For example, when you say "no" to a dominant *Brown* do you know what they actually hear? They hear "maybe." The *Brown* thinks to herself,

"Well, I just wasn't persistent enough."

*or*

"I need to come at this differently with more information."

*or*

"I'll talk to someone else."

So when a *Brown* says "no" to you, their expectation is that you'll come back again if it's important or you'll provide more compelling reasons. The word "no" for them is often a quick way to test for resolution—not a final demand.

## STEREOTYPE: "BLUE-STYLE COMMUNICATORS ARE HIGH MAINTENANCE CRYBABIES."

We observe a *Blue* emoting and determine that all they want to do is complain. Not so. *Blues* do want to be appreciated and listened to. Often times their real message is simply an indirect request for someone just to tune in and genuinely acknowledge what they are feeling. They aren't asking for you to solve things or to spend a lot of time with them, but to empathize.

> LEARN HOW *BROWNS* USE LANGUAGE TO AVOID THE TRAP OF STYLE STEREOTYPING.

## STEREOTYPE: "GREEN-STYLE COMMUNICATORS ARE ANAL-RETENTIVE NITPICKERS."

We observe their thorough analysis, their tendency to ask many questions and their attention to accuracy and detail. If we do not understand the Green style, we can interpret this as impersonal—even untrusting—"bean counting."

The *Green* simply wants to make sure they are making the best decision. They are focused on quality, not on miring things down. So, if you can provide them with accurate, complete, data and factor in time for their analysis, *Greens* will not only get the job done, but also will do it in a way that minimizes mistakes or re-work.

## STEREOTYPE: "RED-STYLE COMMUNICATORS ARE IRRESPONSIBLE FLAKES."

We observe their non-linear, creative approach to things and their tendency to be drawn to "where the action is." If we do not relate to the Red style, we can interpret this as "flakiness," an inability to follow through.

If you live with or work with a high *Red*, give them deadlines. "No deadline, I've got 16 other things to do." And when the deadline approaches, if you need order and structure in your life—just don't be there to see "how" they get it done. *Reds* often do their best work in what low *Reds* would call "chaotic situations." Again, it's a difference of style, not quality or commitment to follow-through.

> LEARN THAT *BLUES'* EMOTING SOMETIMES IS AN INDIRECT REQUEST FOR YOU TO TUNE IN.

# STYLE-VALUE CONFUSION

Related to style stereotyping is the second trap we sometimes fall into with respect to style. Sometimes we confuse "style" with "values" or character traits such as honesty, courage and compassion.

---

**LEARN THAT *GREENS* WANT TO MAKE THE RIGHT DECISION.**

## EXAMPLES OF THE CONFUSION BETWEEN STYLE AND VALUES[2]

- "Hitler was a *Brown*, wasn't he?"
- "*Blues* are spineless wimps, aren't they?"
- "Those *Greens*—ice water in their veins, robots, right?"
- "Aren't all criminals *Reds*?"

[2]*These are questions often raised during our* Success Signals *workshops.*

---

When we make value judgments like the ones above, we fail to remember that style is only about *how we communicate*, not about *the inner person*. Values like honesty, compassion and courage are part of the inner person. Personality traits such as the ability to see the big picture or follow through on commitments are also part of the inner person. There are "big picture" thinkers and responsible people among all styles.

Certainly there are *Browns* who are honest and *Browns* who are dishonest. Same with *Blues, Reds* and *Greens.* A criminal can be any style. In fact, in work done in prisons and juvenile detention centers we've determined that there are inmates of all styles and no one style predominates. "How" a person goes about committing a crime however, is influenced by dominant color styles.

We are all, to some degree, style bigots. We like our own style and often tend to think it's the superior style. Imagine how you react when another person comes across like they are better than you are. Even subtle signals of superiority can really make you angry, resentful and resistant. Why then would it be any different when the tables are turned?

Whenever you make a negative judgment about another's style, chances are you are transmitting signals of superiority and inadvertently sparking resistance. Sure we all get irritated from time to time when someone drones on and on, or issues ultimatums, complains endlessly or disrupts a conversation.

What we need to be careful of is the tendency to jump from a specific situation to a generalization like "That's the way the *Reds, Greens, Browns* or *Blues* are."

But what if the other person is really extreme in their style? Then what? Most people go to style extremes when they are under a lot of stress. Fortunately, there are some simple things that will help them calm down much of the time.

> LEARN TO GIVE *REDS* DEADLINES SO THEY MEET YOUR TIMELINE NEEDS.

# NOTES

# 8

## Styles in Stress:
## Calming Things Down,
## Clearing Things Up

When we human beings are under consider-
able stress, we tend to communicate in ways
that are extreme expressions of our own
style blend.

Because human beings are a unique blend of all
colors, we engage in all kinds of extreme behaviors when
under stress. However, as you can see in Figure 8-1, our
dominant style tendencies will lead to certain kinds of
extremes.

This chapter will tell you more about how each style
reacts under stress and give you a tool to calm down
many conflict situations.

> "If dogs could talk, we'd
> probably has as much trouble
> getting along with them
> as we do with people."
>
> - Anonymous

# FIGURE 8-1:  STYLE CONFLICT "EXTREMES"

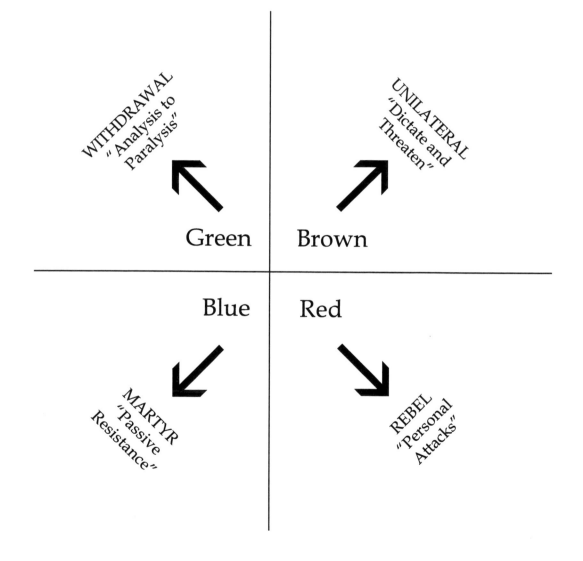

# STYLE EXTREMES

## BROWN AND GREEN

The Brown communicator, when under stress, will tend to become *unilateral*. She will dictate solutions and threaten dire consequences if her instructions are not carried out.

The Green communicator goes in the opposite direction. Literally. While a *Brown* under stress will get "in your face," a *Green* will "turn his back." Green style communicators, in keeping with their conflict-adverse tendencies, *withdraw* under stress — physically, mentally and emotionally. They go off by themselves and engage in "analysis to paralysis," cycling the same data set over and over, unable to act.

A good friend with dominant Green tendencies tells of how arguments with her *Brown* husband would last for hours. He would begin to dictate in his frustration and she would leave the room. "How come every time we argue, you leave the room?" "And your point is…?", my friend would think as she withdrew. Sometimes, she'd be up in the bedroom with the door closed and her husband would still be in the dining room, dictating solutions to their problems.

> UNDER STRESS, *BROWNS* TEND TO BECOME UNILATERAL.

## BLUE

The Blue style communicator — also conflict averse — goes to "martyr" when under stress. "I gave my life-blood to this organization," you can hear them saying. "Do you want to take more? Here, take blood from a stone!"

But does that mean that the *Blues* are helpless in a conflict situation? Not at all. In line with their stress behavior, a Blue style communicator will engage in *passive resistance.* He will go "by the book," especially if the "book" is a safe way to make a point or get revenge.

Years ago I was asked to help resolve a conflict at a large hotel. The housekeeping supervisor had called a staff meeting during which she informed the room attendants that there would be no more overtime in their department.

"You've got a schedule of rooms to clean," she said. "Follow the schedule and get out on time."

When one room attendant asked "What are we supposed to do when people don't leave their rooms and we need to clean them?" the supervisor responded, "Do I have to do the thinking for you? I'm so tired of your whining. Just do it—no more excuses."

Well, the room attendants—most of whom had strong Blue preferences—did just as they were told. And, if a guest was asleep in his bed, he might wake up to see someone dusting around his head. If he stepped out of the shower, he might find a room attendant, busily vacuuming in the other room. If the guest complained, the room attendant would answer, "I'm really sorry, I didn't mean to disturb you, but they gave me this schedule and said I had to follow it."

The supervisor wanted to discipline every last room attendant. Of course, when she realized that they were following her orders to the letter…well, it was clear that they had made their point.

> UNDER STRESS, *GREENS* TEND TO WITHDRAW.

## RED

The Red style under stress becomes the original rebel without a cause. In conflict, Red style communicators hurl *personal attacks.* They really know how to push your buttons.

When *Reds* are stressed out, they often say very provocative and inflammatory things. For them it's a physical release. To others it's a vicious attack. Remember, though, *Reds* are often not literal communicators. Studies show that 24 hours after a *Red* has blown up at you they do not remember 90 percent of what they said, nor did they mean it literally.

*Keep in mind, we are not talking about bad people. We are talking about behaviors under stress — behaviors that do not result in success for the speaker or the listener.*

# How to Calm Things Down to Clear Things Up

You can hardly clear up misunderstandings with these behaviors going on. So what's a person to do?

First and foremost, be realistic. THE ONLY BEHAVIOR WE CAN CONTROL IS OUR OWN.

However, we can often influence others to change their behavior by how we respond and by changing our behavior. That usually means doing the *opposite* of what we want to do when another person behaves in an extreme style.

How does this work?

UNDER STRESS, *BLUES* TEND TO PASSIVELY RESIST.

## THE CALMING TWO-STEP

Here are the two rules to influence another's behavior in conflict situations:

1. Do the opposite of what feels good.
2. Check and moderate your own behavior. Move out of any extremes you may be in. Translate your message into the other person's style or acknowledge their style respectfully.

Perhaps we should explain and illustrate (since these rules may seem counterintuitive to some).

**Do the opposite of what feels good.** When we are in conflict, what feels good to do? Why, relieve stress, of course. And how do we relieve stress? By engaging in our extreme behaviors. This creates a dilemma. The extreme behavior relieves immediate emotional stress for us but only builds up a head of steam in the other person. When we do the opposite of what feels comfortable, we change the dynamic.

**Check and moderate your own behavior.** Translate your message into the other person's style if you can. Do not mimic the other person's style. Stay in your own preferred style, if you want. Just get out of the extreme position. Become milder in your response.

You may be wondering: How would this two-step process look? How does it work?

Here's a story to illustrate:

Ellen has a definite preference for the Red style. Her husband, Mike, prefers a Green way of communicating. One night, Mike comes home from work and he's uncharacteristically quiet.

At dinner Ellen says, "What's the matter, did you have a bad day?"

Mike responds by shrugging his shoulders.

Ellen begins to feel a little annoyed. She continues to ask Mike to tell her what troubles him and Mike stays silent. After dinner, Mike goes into the living room, sits on the couch and puts the newspaper in front of his face.

What does Ellen do? You guessed it. She tears the newspaper away. "I'm talking to you!" she says, at a rather high volume.

Mike gets up and begins to walk down the hall towards the bedroom. Ellen — kicking into extreme Red behavior — follows him, hurling personal attacks. "I didn't get married to live in solitary confinement or talk

> UNDER STRESS, *REDS* TEND TO HURL PERSONAL ATTACKS.

to the walls!" she yells. "I'm sick of your sullen, mopey, arrogant..."

All of a sudden Ellen stops yelling. She flashes on what she learned last week in a workshop. Wait a minute, she thinks. Do the opposite of what feels good. Well, what "feels good" is to follow Mike down the hall and yell insults. It's difficult, but she stops yelling and apologizes.

"Mike, I'm sorry. I didn't mean to provoke a fight. I know I came on too strong. I was just worried about you and wanted to know if I could help."

"Well, you sure have a funny way of showing it!" Mike has turned around now and is looking at her.

"Gee," Ellen thinks to herself, "he's actually talking to me." So she responds calmly and quietly: "I know that I was out of line with what I said. But, Honey, I was truly worried. You were so quiet. I thought that something was wrong."

> REMEMBER... THE ONLY BEHAVIOR YOU CAN CONTROL IS YOUR OWN.

This calm approach does the trick. Mike begins walking with her back to the living room where he tells her about his frustrating day.

## WHY DOES THIS WORK?

This approach *does* work for two very basic reasons:

1. When you stop engaging in extreme behaviors, you are giving the other person some emotional "breathing room." When you are both acting from an extreme place, you are cornering and driving each other deeper and deeper into behaviors designed to relieve immediate stress. By stopping and moderating, you shift the dynamic and give the other person an opportunity to come out of their extreme "corner."

2. By the very act of *thinking* about your behavior, you go from a visceral emotional reaction (controlled by your limbic system, your "dinosaur

brain") to a more intellectual approach (allowing your prefrontal lobe to process your emotions). This enables you to respond more accurately to the other person's signals in a given situation. It helps you send the kind of signals that they may respond to.

Of course, no approach is foolproof and this technique is not SUFFICIENT WITH PEOPLE WHO ARE MENTALLY UNSTABLE, VIOLENT, OR UNDER THE INFLUENCE OF DRUGS/ALCOHOL. WHEN IN CONFLICT SITUATIONS WITH SUCH PEOPLE, GET AWAY FROM THE SITUATION. DO NOT TRY TO INFLUENCE UNLESS TRAINED PROFESSIONALLY TO DO SO.

## CONCLUSION

Although we are capable of all kinds of extreme behavior, people tend to use the extreme behavior that is in concert with their preferred communication style more often. It is important to understand that you are not dealing with a bad person in such a situation but with nonproductive behavior.

You can calm things down by following our simple two-step process. This process allows you to send more successful signals while allowing the other person some emotional "space" to calm their own behavior.

Remember our *Green* friend who left the room every time her *Brown* husband began to dictate? She learned that all she had to do was stay in the room for a few minutes, nodding and silent. Inevitably, her *Brown* husband would come to a stopping point and say in a much calmer voice, "Do you understand?" "Yes," she'd answer. "Yes, I do understand that you're upset. I am, too. Could we bring the conversation down a notch so that I can really hear you?" Fighting time cut by 80 percent. She considers it well worth hanging in there.

> THE CALMING TWO-STEP:
> 1. DO THE OPPOSITE OF WHAT FEELS GOOD.
> 2. MODIFY YOUR OWN BEHAVIOR.

FIGURE 8-2: THE CALMING TWO-STEP

To influence another's extreme behaviors:

1. Do the opposite of what feels good to you.

2. Check your own behavior and move out of any extremes you may be in. Translate your message into the other person's style, or acknowledge it respectfully.

# Examples:

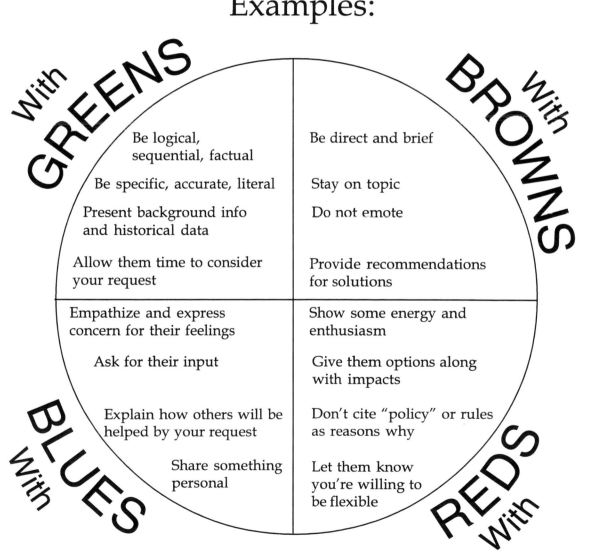

# NOTES

# 9

# Who's Who Out There?
# Determining Others' Style

So how do you know what style another person is using at any given moment?

There are ways to determine someone's communication style. None of them, however, will work well if we pigeonhole people and expect them to always communicate in one dominant color style. That's because all human beings are a complex blend of color styles and their associated signals. We need to keep in mind that while we all have tendencies to use certain styles and signals more than others, we do communicate in all of the styles to some extent. The important thing to be able to determine then is what style a person is in at a particular time. There are three ways to make such an assessment:

> *"I observe myself, and I come to know others."*
>
> *- Lao-Tzu (604-531 B.C.)*

> ✔ OBSERVE
> ✔ ASK
> ✔ EXPERIMENT

# OBSERVE

We all need to become better style observers in order to send success signals. What are we observing?

- The words that people use
- Their general demeanor and affect as they speak with us, and
- The way they react to our attempts to "speak their language"

TO DETERMINE WHAT STYLE A PERSON IS IN AT ANY GIVEN POINT:
- OBSERVE
- ASK
- EXPERIMENT

## BROWN SIGNALS

What are some signs that an individual is speaking Brown?

- Use of short, direct sentences
- Closed-ended questions (ones which require you to answer either "yes" or "no")
- Words that tell you to get to the point
  - "What's your point?"
  - "Get to the bottom line"
  - "Cut to the chase"
- An impatience with detail
- A lack of "feeling" words
- Multi-tasking while speaking with you

## GREEN SIGNALS

How about Green?

- A desire to get into the details of the topic
- Longer, more complex sentences
- Requests for written materials, especially in advance of the meeting
- Lots of questions to clarify or get more data
- Understated demeanor and unemotional tone
- Words that indicate a need for detail, logic, research and planning.
  - "How can you prove this?"

- "On what research do you base your recommendation?"
- "In what context are you speaking?"
- "Let me think about that"

## BLUE SIGNALS

And Blue?

- Begins the conversation with personal inquiries
  - "How have you been?"
  - "How was your weekend?"
  - "How's your family?"
- Talks in the language of feelings
  - "Here is how I feel about the situation. How do you feel? Tell me honestly."
- Demeanor shows a range of emotions
- Asks questions about how other people might be affected by the topic you are discussing
- Asks if you have consulted the affected people in a decision-making situation

> OBSERVE THE PERSON'S WORDS, DEMEANOR AND REACTIONS TO YOU TO DETERMINE THEIR STYLE.

## RED SIGNALS

And Red?

- Non-sequential in their approach to a topic
- Tells stories or gives testimonials to support their point
- Demeanor is dramatic, often upbeat
- Talk is often fast-paced
- Tells jokes and uses humor frequently
- Over-generalizes
  - "You *always* break your promises"
- Uses exaggeration to make a point
  - "That wine was the worst ever made on this planet!" = "I didn't like that wine"

To improve your observation skills, watch television sitcoms occasionally. They often depict people in one style interacting with others in very different styles. Remember the show "Murphy Brown"? Candice Bergen played Murphy in a very "Brown" manner, did she not?

What if you are observing and are still not sure? Or you want to know straight away what kind of style you are dealing with?

> WE ALL NEED TO BECOME BETTER STYLE OBSERVERS IN ORDER TO SEND SUCCESS SIGNALS.

# ASK.

Now, if the other person has not read this book or been to a *Success Signals* workshop, they may look at you funny if you ask whether they're speaking Green. So, instead, ask a question based on the behavior you see. For example:

## BROWN

- **"It sounds like you want to get this solved right away. Want me to get to the bottom line?"** (Translation: Are you speaking Brown right now?)

- If you get this answer…"No. Why don't you start over, take it from the top and give me more details"…chances are the person is *not* speaking Brown!

- If the answer is: "You got it!" Then get to the bottom line fast!

## GREEN

- **"You seem to have a lot of questions. Would you like me to get you a report on this? Or should I start over from the beginning?"** (Translation: Are you speaking Green right now?)

- If you get this answer... "No, actually, my questions are about how the staff feels about it"...the person is not speaking Green.
- If the answer you get is: "Actually, I'd like you to start over from the beginning now *and* send me a report to read before our next meeting"...bingo! They're definitely speaking Green.

## BLUE

- **"Before I continue, let me ask: are you okay with what I'm saying? How are you feeling about it?"** (Translation: Are you speaking Blue?)
- If you get this answer... "I'm mainly feeling like I'd like you to get to the point"...probably not "Blue."
- If the answer you get is: "Actually, I *am* feeling concerned about your message. Can we talk about it a little more?"...It's time to explore your listener's feelings.

## RED

- **"This doesn't look like it's lighting your fire...am I right?"** (Translation: Are you speaking Red?)
- If you get the answer... "I don't have *a fire*. I have thoughts on the matter"...don't continue along this vein. Go Green.
- If the answer you get is: "Right on. Let's boogie..." that's a "Red" telling you to liven up the presentation.

LEARN EACH STYLE'S UNIQUE SIGNALS AND ADAPT YOUR SIGNALS ACCORDINGLY.

# EXPERIMENT (IF OBSERVING AND ASKING FAIL)

I once had an interview with a CEO of a large company about a labor-management consulting project. Never having met him before I decided to start by sending Brown signals.

I quickly ticked off three things my company could do to help him get results. He looked at me and said, "In what context are you speaking?"

I should have picked up his Green signal but instead I thought to myself, "Well, he's not that Brown. I'll try Blue."

"We can make a difference in terms of improved morale, productivity and positive working relationships," I replied.

"What's the relevance here?" he shot back.

Finally the light went on and I started sending Green signals. Less than a minute later he looked at me and said, "Now you're singing my tune" — a strong indicator that I was communicating in his preferred style. By doing so did that mean he would hire me? Not necessarily. What it did mean was that he was receptive to listening to me. Getting others to really tune in and listen to us is a powerful agent for success in any setting.

> GETTING OTHERS TO REALLY LISTEN IS A POWERFUL AGENT FOR SUCCESS IN ANY SETTING.

# NOTES

# NOTES

# 10

# Success is a Rainbow of Signals

## APPRECIATE ALL STYLES

Imagine, for a moment, an organization with no *Brown*. What would be missing?

How about:

- Results
- Practical approaches
- Follow through
- Real-time decision making
- Helpful structures and rules

And if there were no *Green?*

That organization would have no:

- Planning
- Thoroughness
- Accuracy
- Attention to quality
- Logical analysis

> *"When we seek to discover the best in others, we somehow bring out the best in ourselves."*
>
> *- William Arthur Ward*

No *Blue?*

Gone would be:

- Team building
- Inclusiveness
- Compassion
- Collaboration
- Helpfulness and support

And no *Red*?

Missing:

- Energy
- Excitement
- Creativity
- Spontaneity
- Willingness to "push the envelope"

> ORGANIZATIONS AND RELATIONSHIPS THAT DON'T EMBRACE ALL STYLES QUICKLY BECOME DYSFUNCTIONAL.

Can you picture missing any one of these colors? Organizations and relationships that don't embrace all styles quickly become dysfunctional. In any role you have at home, at work, or in your community you can be more successful when you draw on the full spectrum of color styles and signals.

I'll never forget the advice my husband gave me when I was just starting my business. In fact, I believe it was and still is the single most helpful thing anyone has said to me about my work effort. And because he delivered this advice in my dominant style—not his—I really listened and acted on it.

What happened?

Soon after I opened my business a decade ago my husband came to me and expressed enthusiasm and support for my new venture. "I think you have a lot to offer and can really make a difference." Yes! My Red side liked hearing that.

Then he followed up with, "But if you don't change the way you handle money the IRS will shut you down or you'll go bankrupt." That really got through to my Brown side.

A little background: My husband and I always had very different approaches to finance. Having a lot of Green in his style he's always known exactly how much money he had. Me, I never used to open my bank statements unless there was "pink" in the window of the envelope. Even then, I'd let them sit around for a while. I did have a system. I'd try to remember to record each check written in a check registry and then once a month I'd throw in about $5 for bank service charges and figure that was close enough. Eventually I would get so hopelessly out of balance that I'd just change banks and start over. To my husband this was like committing a felony.

After his Red-Brown advice on my business, I hired an accountant and a bookkeeper to set up and maintain the financial systems and make sure we paid our taxes and bills and invoiced on time.

At first it was a pain for me to even review the financial statements, but after 10 or 12 months something happened. Those numbers were showing me patterns—who our repeat clients were, which products and services were most in demand—all that Green detail was now providing me insight into how to strengthen and grow the business. To this day, I don't think I would have followed my husband's advice if he hadn't communicated in my style, and as a result, I wouldn't have the level of professional success I now enjoy. So when you're tempted to dismiss style as superficial or not important, ask yourself "How can I succeed if I don't get my intended message across?"

> DON'T DISMISS THE IMPORTANCE OF STYLE. HOW CAN YOU SUCCEED IF YOU DON'T GET YOUR INTENDED MESSAGE ACROSS?

# CONCLUSION

How do you send Success Signals more and more of the time?

1. Understand your own style preferences and the impact they have on others;

2. Learn about styles that are different from yours;

3. Appreciate others' styles and learn how to more easily speak their languages;

4. Remember that you have access to *all* four "colors" and don't hesitate to bring up the style that will help clarify the signals between you and another person, when needed; and

5. See beyond style to the substance of those you work with, play with and live with.

> ONLY WHEN YOU APPRECIATE STYLE DIFFERENCES CAN YOU SEND SUCCESS SIGNALS.

# NOTES

# NOTES

# 11

# Questions Frequently Asked About Success Signals

**Q** When you tell me to approach someone in his/her style language, isn't that manipulative?

**A** Remember, style is "how" a message is sent not the message itself. So when communicating with someone who uses another language how is it manipulative to speak in his/her native tongue? So, if I know how to speak Japanese and you are a Japanese-speaking person, I would probably be more successful getting my message across by speaking Japanese, wouldn't I?

We are all multilingual when it comes to style languages. We have access to all of the "colors." So, even if we are not particularly fluent in a certain style, we can still use it. So why not send advanced materials to someone who favors a Green way of communicating? Why not get right to the point for a *Brown?* Why not approach a *Blue* with a personal reference or a *Red* with a joke?

> *"The best of life is conversation, and the greatest success is confidence, or perfect understanding between sincere people."*
>
> *- Emerson*

Are some colors better matches for love and marriage than others are?

 There is no research to suggest that partners need to have the same — or even similar — styles. Understanding and appreciation are the foundations of any good relationship and this goes for style, as well. If you can respect the style of your significant other — if you can appreciate how his or her style complements your own — then you have the makings of a productive relationship.

> RESEARCHERS AGREE THAT WE HAVE DEVELOPED STYLE PREFERENCES AT LEAST BY THE TIME WE ARE FIVE OR SIX YEARS OLD.

 How do we get our style — are we born with it or do we learn it?

 While there are various theories about the genesis of style, we don't really know whether it's genetically programmed, shaped by our environment or some combination of the two. Researchers in this area do agree that we have developed style preferences at least by the time we are five or six years old. Life is a journey, though. As we discover more about ourselves as we grow and experience new situations, we also learn more about our unique communication styles. So, although you will likely have enduring style preferences, don't put yourself into a "style box." Learn to experience all of your "colors!"

I'm more of one color at work and more of another at home. Am I schizophrenic?

 No, that's entirely normal. Different experiences bring out different styles in us. We also employ styles that, hopefully, are most effective for us and for others in particular situations. For example, you may have a preference to communicate in the Blue style. However, when your child needs a strong hand, you may kick into Brown. Your parental instincts tell you that a Brown approach will be most helpful in this situation.

> THE MOST EFFECTIVE TEAMS AND ORGANIZATIONS NEED *ALL* STYLES TO BE SUCCESSFUL.

 Should we select people for employment based on their style?

 Although people may be naturally drawn to certain lines of work because of their style preferences, it would be a mistake to screen people of diverse styles out of certain jobs. In addition to the talent you would miss by doing this, the fact is that successful teams and organizations need *all* styles to be successful.

 Are women more apt to be dominant *Blues* and men dominant *Browns* in their approach to communicating?

 Even though in our culture women are often expected to act *Blue* (sensitive, emotive) and men are expected to act *Brown* (strong, commanding) our research clearly shows that there is no gender difference when it comes to style. All styles are equally used by men and women.

**Q** When I figure out someone's main color preference can I be assured they will consistently use that color style?

**A** When we first learn the Success Signals system, we can sometimes put people into style "boxes." We act as if a person with a particular dominant style *is that way all the time.* This misses the point that everyone is both unique, complex and multidimensional in terms of style.

Remember that style is a language.

...and we are *all* multilingual. None of us is one way all the time. We are all blends of different styles.

1. For one thing, rarely is someone speaking purely deep Blue to you. If you listen, you will hear shades of Red or Brown or Green. Do not assume that you cannot express your feelings to someone who has a predominant Brown tendency. They have Blue in their style, too.

2. Different situations will tend to bring out different styles in an individual. Someone can speak Brown/Green at work and speak Blue to his spouse.

Treating styles as a language can help you send success signals in personal and professional situations. When you are on a team whose members know the Success Signals system, you can tell your co-workers something like this: "I need to be more Brown... that report is due by noon!" Sending a signal like this can avoid misunderstandings and hurt feelings as you stay focused, quiet and on task.

> TREATING STYLES AS A LANGUAGE CAN HELP YOU SEND SUCCESS SIGNALS IN PERSONAL AND PROFESSIONAL SITUATIONS.

Where can I learn more about how to use my style effectively?

 Here are some options:

1. Contact Agreement Dynamics, Inc. for information on Success Signals workshops available in your area:

   TOLL FREE:   1-800-97-AGREE
                1-800-972-4733
        TEL:   (206) 546-8048
   EMAIL: hq@agreementdynamics.com

   AGREEMENT DYNAMICS
   PO BOX 33640
   SEATTLE, WA 98133

   ---

   EMAIL US YOUR
   QUESTIONS AT

   *hq@agreementdynamics.com*

2. Visit us online at www.agreementdynamics.com for information on our videotape of Success Signals. Visit the website periodically for updates of our Success Signals products (including online tools) as well as other related programs and products.

# NOTES

# 12
## Suggested Reading

- *Discovering Your Personality Type*
  By Don Richard Riso

- *Getting Together*
  By Roger Fisher and Scott Brown

- *Leadership, Team Building, Self-Esteem and Conflict Resolution Communication*
  By Stefan Neilson and Shay Thoelke

- *The Luscher Color Test*
  By Ian Scott and Dr. Max Luscher

- *Managing Your Mind*
  By Gillian Butler and Tony Hope

- *Multiple Intelligences*
  By Howard Gardner

- *Personal Styles and Effective Performance*
  By David W. Merrill and Roger H. Reid

- *The Personality Compass*
  By Diane Turner and Thelma Greco

- *Seven Kinds of Smart*
  By Thomas Armstrong

- *Whole Brain Thinking*
  By Jacquelyn Wonder and Priscilla Donovan

*As of publication of this book, more than 100,000 people have attended Agreement Dynamics' Success Signals workshop.*

# NOTES

# 13

# Appendix

This Appendix contains:

- Answers to Page 27, *Test Your Knowledge*
- Agreement Dynamics: Who We Are
- Additional Success Signals Profiles
- Agreement Dynamics Products and Order Form
- Color Cards

> "From my experience, when failure is not an option, you call Agreement Dynamics. No question about it."
>
> – Phil Kushlan, Executive Director, Washington Public Stadium Authority, 1999

| | Blue | Brown | Green | Red |
|---|---|---|---|---|
| A. "Don't be cruel to a heart that's true." | (Blue) | Brown | Green | Red |
| B. "A stitch in time saves nine." | Blue | Brown | (Green) | Red |
| C. "Hit the road, Jack." | Blue | (Brown) | Green | Red |
| D. "I left my heart in San Francisco." | (Blue) | Brown | Green | Red |
| E. "I did it my way." | Blue | (Brown) | Green | Red |
| F. "Look before you leap." | Blue | Brown | (Green) | Red |
| G. "I'm so excited." | Blue | Brown | Green | (Red) |
| H. "Fifty ways to leave your lover." | Blue | Brown | (Green) | Red |
| I. "Don't mess with Texas!" | Blue | (Brown) | Green | Red |
| J. "Light my fire." | Blue | Brown | Green | (Red) |
| K. "People who need people." | (Blue) | Brown | Green | Red |
| L. "Let me ride…under sunny skies above/don't fence me in." | Blue | Brown | Green | (Red) |

# AGREEMENT DYNAMICS: COMPANY PROFILE

Agreement Dynamics, Inc. helps individuals, groups and organizations forge successful relationships, agreements and *results*.

When Agreement Dynamics was founded in 1991, it was a one-woman shop, primarily providing conflict resolution and negotiation consulting, facilitation and training services. Today, Agreement Dynamics has a diverse group of highly successful specialists in virtually all areas of individual and organizational development. We have had the privilege of working with over 400 organizations in both the public and private sectors in the U.S., Canada and Europe. While our closely-knit team of employees and colleagues comes from varied backgrounds, we are all focused on bringing the most effective tools to our clients.

> *"Agreement Dynamics is in a league of their own. Using their tools has done more for the Port of Seattle to build positive, constructive employee and customer relations than any other method we've tried."*
>
> *– John Swanson, Director of Labor Relations, Port of Seattle, 1986-2000*

# WHO WE ARE:

**Rhonda Hilyer**, Founder and President
**Dee Endelman**, Senior Associate
**Ginny Ratliff**, Executive Director
**Other Staff and Associates**:

Agreement Dynamics has a diverse team of consultants, trainers, facilitators and experts to serve a variety of client requests, including: training in interpersonal communication and negotiations, labor-management relations, retreat facilitation, team building, management/team coaching, personal empowerment, change management, facilitation of multi-party stakeholder negotiations and workplace violence prevention.

# WORKSHOPS

Our trainings are compelling, effective and designed to be immediately useful to participants. Current workshops include:

## SUCCESS SIGNALS: USING YOUR COMMUNICATION STYLE EFFECTIVELY

A class designed to teach you more about your unique style and help you send success signals to people of *all* styles.

## LEADERSHIP STYLE MAKES A DIFFERENCE

Get that "magic touch" which great leaders seem to have. We call it "style versatility" and it *can* be learned.

## RESOLVE TO CREATE BETTER RELATIONSHIPS AND RESULTS

Learn the secrets of solving problems and resolving conflicts in a way that makes your relationships stronger and more creative.

## RESOLVE TO NEGOTIATE GREAT AGREEMENTS

This workshop is designed specifically for labor and management to get more of what each wants out of contract negotiations — including a healthier working relationship.

## YOU ARE THE FACILITATOR

This workshop provides basic facilitation skills that can help you help groups achieve great results together!

> "It's (Success Signals workshop) very easy to retain and you feel that you can use it immediately. That's what we found individually and across the employee base.... It automatically became a part of the vocabulary here at Washington Dental Service... It's a fun way of thinking of something which could otherwise be an irritation."
>
> - Tracy Peterson,
> Vice President of Public Affairs and External Relations,
> Washington Dental Service

## CHANGE HAPPENS!

How to survive and thrive in the midst of personal changes.

## YOUR EMPOWERMENT TOOLKIT

How can you live your hopes instead of your fears? With a set of tools that you can use to claim your personal power in difficult situations.

## WALKING THE TALK OF CUSTOMER SERVICE: THREE STEPS THAT WILL TAKE YOU MILES

This is the personal side of customer service. What do customers expect from you and how can you deliver in a way that makes *you* a superstar? Learn and practice the three steps.

# CONSULTING AND FACILITATING

*"As a professional conference organizer, I have heard many, many speakers. Yours are exceptional and highly sought after by both my audiences and my curriculum committee."*

*- Pat Murtaugh, Assistant Executive Director for Conventions and Education, National Association of Fleet Administrators*

We have provided consulting and facilitation services to hundreds of organizations, in both public and private sectors and to every level within (and between) organizations.

Working collaboratively with clients, we offer years of experience and expertise in the following areas:

- Conflict resolution;
- Collaborative labor relations;
- Organizational change;
- Management and team coaching;
- Multi-party problem solving and negotiations;
- Design and facilitation of retreats and strategic planning sessions;
- Communications;
- Team building.

# Success Signals Profile

INSTRUCTIONS: Place a check by each word that is **really** like you. If the meaning of the word is unclear, do not place a check by it. After you've completed the Profile, turn the page upside down to tally your score.

___ accountable (w)
___ accuracy (z)
___ achievement (w)
___ adventurer (x)
___ agreeable (y)
___ amiable (y)
___ analytical (z)
___ asks (y)
___ authority (w)
___ avoids conflict (y)
___ being accepted (y)
___ being in control (w)
___ bottom line (w)
___ budgets (z)
___ careful (z)
___ cautious action (z)
___ challenge authority (x)
___ conceptual (z)
___ conforming (y)
___ considerate (y)
___ creative (x)
___ decisive (w)
___ demanding (w)
___ dependable (y)
___ detail oriented (z)
___ direct (w)
___ discipline (w)
___ do it now (w)
___ down with routine (x)
___ dramatic (x)
___ driver (w)
___ dutiful (w)
___ efficient (w)
___ emotional (y)
___ enthusiastic (x)
___ exacting (z)
___ excitable (x)
___ exciting (x)
___ fast (x)
___ feelings first (y)
___ flamboyant (x)
___ flashy (x)
___ flexible (x)
___ freedom (x)
___ friendly (y)
___ fun (x)
___ future focus (x)
___ gestures (x)
___ giving (y)
___ harmonious (y)
___ helps others (y)
___ history (z)
___ honest feelings (y)
___ impatient (w)
___ implementer (w)
___ impulsive (x)
___ innovative (z)
___ law & order (w)
___ leader (w)
___ lighthearted (x)
___ likes change (x)
___ link together (y)
___ listening (y)
___ literal (z)
___ logical (z)
___ loving (y)
___ loyal (y)
___ mastery (z)
___ mover (x)
___ orderly (z)
___ organized (z)
___ originality (x)
___ patient (z)
___ people centered (y)
___ perfectionist (z)
___ performer (x)
___ planner (z)
___ playful (x)
___ powerful (w)
___ practical (w)
___ precise (z)
___ predicts (z)
___ prepared (w)
___ present focused (y)
___ prioritizes (z)
___ probing (z)
___ quality (z)
___ questioning (z)
___ rapid reaction (x)
___ relater (y)
___ responsible (w)
___ results oriented (w)
___ risk taker (x)
___ romantic (y)
___ saving (w)
___ sensitive (y)
___ sentimental (y)
___ serious (z)
___ skeptical (z)
___ spends (x)
___ spontaneous (x)
___ spurt worker (x)
___ status (w)
___ stimulating (x)
___ strategist (z)
___ strong-willed (w)
___ structure (w)
___ supportive (y)
___ sympathetic (y)
___ take charge (w)
___ team oriented (y)
___ tells (w)
___ theoretical (z)
___ thinker (z)
___ tough (w)
___ traditional (w)
___ warmth (y)
___ willing (y)
___ works best alone (z)
___ zestful (x)

Total up the number of checks you've placed next to words with the "w," "x," "y" or "z" notation. Refer to chapter 3, page 38 in *Success Signals* for the KEY to this Profile.

___ "w" words ___ "x" words ___ "y" words ___ "z" words


Agreement Dynamics • P.O. Box 33640, Seattle, WA 98133 • U.S.A.
www.agreementdynamics.com
Phone: (206) 546-8048

# Success Signals Profile

INSTRUCTIONS: Place a check by each word that is **really** like you. If the meaning of the word is unclear, do not place a check by it. After you've completed the Profile, turn the page upside down to tally your score.

| | | | |
|---|---|---|---|
| ___ accountable (w) | ___ driver (w) | ___ likes change (x) | ___ responsible (w) |
| ___ accuracy (z) | ___ dutiful (w) | ___ link together (y) | ___ results oriented (w) |
| ___ achievement (w) | ___ efficient (w) | ___ listening (y) | ___ risk taker (x) |
| ___ adventurer (x) | ___ emotional (y) | ___ literal (z) | ___ romantic (y) |
| ___ agreeable (y) | ___ enthusiastic (x) | ___ logical (z) | ___ saving (w) |
| ___ amiable (y) | ___ exacting (z) | ___ loving (y) | ___ sensitive (y) |
| ___ analytical (z) | ___ excitable (x) | ___ loyal (y) | ___ sentimental (y) |
| ___ asks (y) | ___ exciting (x) | ___ mastery (z) | ___ serious (z) |
| ___ authority (w) | ___ fast (x) | ___ mover (x) | ___ skeptical (z) |
| ___ avoids conflict (y) | ___ feelings first (y) | ___ orderly (z) | ___ spends (x) |
| ___ being accepted (y) | ___ flamboyant (x) | ___ organized (z) | ___ spontaneous (x) |
| ___ being in control (w) | ___ flashy (x) | ___ originality (x) | ___ spurt worker (x) |
| ___ bottom line (w) | ___ flexible (x) | ___ patient (z) | ___ status (w) |
| ___ budgets (z) | ___ freedom (x) | ___ people centered (y) | ___ stimulating (x) |
| ___ careful (z) | ___ friendly (y) | ___ perfectionist (z) | ___ strategist (z) |
| ___ cautious action (z) | ___ fun (x) | ___ performer (x) | ___ strong-willed (w) |
| ___ challenge authority (x) | ___ future focus (x) | ___ planner (z) | ___ structure (w) |
| ___ conceptual (z) | ___ gestures (x) | ___ playful (x) | ___ supportive (y) |
| ___ conforming (y) | ___ giving (y) | ___ powerful (w) | ___ sympathetic (y) |
| ___ considerate (y) | ___ harmonious (y) | ___ practical (w) | ___ take charge (w) |
| ___ creative (x) | ___ helps others (y) | ___ precise (z) | ___ team oriented (y) |
| ___ decisive (w) | ___ history (z) | ___ predicts (z) | ___ tells (w) |
| ___ demanding (w) | ___ honest feelings (y) | ___ prepared (w) | ___ theoretical (z) |
| ___ dependable (y) | ___ impatient (w) | ___ present focused (y) | ___ thinker (z) |
| ___ detail oriented (z) | ___ implementer (w) | ___ prioritizes (z) | ___ tough (w) |
| ___ direct (w) | ___ impulsive (x) | ___ probing (z) | ___ traditional (w) |
| ___ discipline (w) | ___ innovative (z) | ___ quality (z) | ___ warmth (y) |
| ___ do it now (w) | ___ law & order (w) | ___ questioning (z) | ___ willing (y) |
| ___ down with routine (x) | ___ leader (w) | ___ rapid reaction (x) | ___ works best alone (z) |
| ___ dramatic (x) | ___ lighthearted (x) | ___ relater (y) | ___ zestful (x) |

Total up the number of checks you've placed next to words with the "w," "x," "y," or "z" notation. Refer to chapter 3, page 38 in *Success Signals* for the KEY to this Profile.

___ "w" words    ___ "x" words    ___ "y" words    ___ "z" words

# Success Signals Profile

INSTRUCTIONS: Place a check by each word that is **really** like you. If the meaning of the word is unclear, do not place a check by it. After you've completed the Profile, turn the page upside down to tally your score.

| | | | |
|---|---|---|---|
| ____ accountable (w) | ____ driver (w) | ____ likes change (x) | ____ responsible (w) |
| ____ accuracy (z) | ____ dutiful (w) | ____ link together (y) | ____ results oriented (w) |
| ____ achievement (w) | ____ efficient (w) | ____ listening (y) | ____ risk taker (x) |
| ____ adventurer (x) | ____ emotional (y) | ____ literal (z) | ____ romantic (y) |
| ____ agreeable (y) | ____ enthusiastic (x) | ____ logical (z) | ____ saving (w) |
| ____ amiable (y) | ____ exacting (z) | ____ loving (y) | ____ sensitive (y) |
| ____ analytical (z) | ____ excitable (x) | ____ loyal (y) | ____ sentimental (y) |
| ____ asks (y) | ____ exciting (x) | ____ mastery (z) | ____ serious (z) |
| ____ authority (w) | ____ fast (x) | ____ mover (x) | ____ skeptical (z) |
| ____ avoids conflict (y) | ____ feelings first (y) | ____ orderly (z) | ____ spends (x) |
| ____ being accepted (y) | ____ flamboyant (x) | ____ organized (z) | ____ spontaneous (x) |
| ____ being in control (w) | ____ flashy (x) | ____ originality (x) | ____ spurt worker (x) |
| ____ bottom line (w) | ____ flexible (x) | ____ patient (z) | ____ status (w) |
| ____ budgets (z) | ____ freedom (x) | ____ people centered (y) | ____ stimulating (x) |
| ____ careful (z) | ____ friendly (y) | ____ perfectionist (z) | ____ strategist (z) |
| ____ cautious action (z) | ____ fun (x) | ____ performer (x) | ____ strong-willed (w) |
| ____ challenge authority (x) | ____ future focus (x) | ____ planner (z) | ____ structure (w) |
| ____ conceptual (z) | ____ gestures (x) | ____ playful (x) | ____ supportive (y) |
| ____ conforming (y) | ____ giving (y) | ____ powerful (w) | ____ sympathetic (y) |
| ____ considerate (y) | ____ harmonious (y) | ____ practical (w) | ____ take charge (w) |
| ____ creative (x) | ____ helps others (y) | ____ precise (z) | ____ team oriented (y) |
| ____ decisive (w) | ____ history (z) | ____ predicts (z) | ____ tells (w) |
| ____ demanding (w) | ____ honest feelings (y) | ____ prepared (w) | ____ theoretical (z) |
| ____ dependable (y) | ____ impatient (w) | ____ present focused (y) | ____ thinker (z) |
| ____ detail oriented (z) | ____ implementer (w) | ____ prioritizes (z) | ____ tough (w) |
| ____ direct (w) | ____ impulsive (x) | ____ probing (z) | ____ traditional (w) |
| ____ discipline (w) | ____ innovative (z) | ____ quality (z) | ____ warmth (y) |
| ____ do it now (w) | ____ law & order (w) | ____ questioning (z) | ____ willing (y) |
| ____ down with routine (x) | ____ leader (w) | ____ rapid reaction (x) | ____ works best alone (z) |
| ____ dramatic (x) | ____ lighthearted (x) | ____ relater (y) | ____ zestful (x) |

____ "w" words     ____ "x" words     ____ "y" words     ____ "z" words

Total up the number of checks you've placed next to words with the "w," "x," "y," or "z" notation. Refer to chapter 3, page 38 in *Success Signals* for the KEY to this Profile.

# Success Signals Profile

INSTRUCTIONS: Place a check by each word that is **really** like you. If the meaning of the word is unclear, do not place a check by it. After you've completed the Profile, turn the page upside down to tally your score.

| | | | |
|---|---|---|---|
| ____ accountable (w) | ____ driver (w) | ____ likes change (x) | ____ responsible (w) |
| ____ accuracy (z) | ____ dutiful (w) | ____ link together (y) | ____ results oriented (w) |
| ____ achievement (w) | ____ efficient (w) | ____ listening (y) | ____ risk taker (x) |
| ____ adventurer (x) | ____ emotional (y) | ____ literal (z) | ____ romantic (y) |
| ____ agreeable (y) | ____ enthusiastic (x) | ____ logical (z) | ____ saving (w) |
| ____ amiable (y) | ____ exacting (z) | ____ loving (y) | ____ sensitive (y) |
| ____ analytical (z) | ____ excitable (x) | ____ loyal (y) | ____ sentimental (y) |
| ____ asks (y) | ____ exciting (x) | ____ mastery (z) | ____ serious (z) |
| ____ authority (w) | ____ fast (x) | ____ mover (x) | ____ skeptical (z) |
| ____ avoids conflict (y) | ____ feelings first (y) | ____ orderly (z) | ____ spends (x) |
| ____ being accepted (y) | ____ flamboyant (x) | ____ organized (z) | ____ spontaneous (x) |
| ____ being in control (w) | ____ flashy (x) | ____ originality (x) | ____ spurt worker (x) |
| ____ bottom line (w) | ____ flexible (x) | ____ patient (z) | ____ status (w) |
| ____ budgets (z) | ____ freedom (x) | ____ people centered (y) | ____ stimulating (x) |
| ____ careful (z) | ____ friendly (y) | ____ perfectionist (z) | ____ strategist (z) |
| ____ cautious action (z) | ____ fun (x) | ____ performer (x) | ____ strong-willed (w) |
| ____ challenge authority (x) | ____ future focus (x) | ____ planner (z) | ____ structure (w) |
| ____ conceptual (z) | ____ gestures (x) | ____ playful (x) | ____ supportive (y) |
| ____ conforming (y) | ____ giving (y) | ____ powerful (w) | ____ sympathetic (y) |
| ____ considerate (y) | ____ harmonious (y) | ____ practical (w) | ____ take charge (w) |
| ____ creative (x) | ____ helps others (y) | ____ precise (z) | ____ team oriented (y) |
| ____ decisive (w) | ____ history (z) | ____ predicts (z) | ____ tells (w) |
| ____ demanding (w) | ____ honest feelings (y) | ____ prepared (w) | ____ theoretical (z) |
| ____ dependable (y) | ____ impatient (w) | ____ present focused (y) | ____ thinker (z) |
| ____ detail oriented (z) | ____ implementer (w) | ____ prioritizes (z) | ____ tough (w) |
| ____ direct (w) | ____ impulsive (x) | ____ probing (z) | ____ traditional (w) |
| ____ discipline (w) | ____ innovative (z) | ____ quality (z) | ____ warmth (y) |
| ____ do it now (w) | ____ law & order (w) | ____ questioning (z) | ____ willing (y) |
| ____ down with routine (x) | ____ leader (w) | ____ rapid reaction (x) | ____ works best alone (z) |
| ____ dramatic (x) | ____ lighthearted (x) | ____ relater (y) | ____ zestful (x) |

Total up the number of checks you've placed next to words with the "w," "x," "y" or "z" notation. Refer to chapter 3, page 38 in *Success Signals* for the KEY to this Profile.

____ "w" words   ____ "x" words   ____ "y" words   ____ "z" words

# Success Signals Profile

INSTRUCTIONS: Place a check by each word that is **really** like you. If the meaning of the word is unclear, do not place a check by it. After you've completed the Profile, turn the page upside down to tally your score.

| | | | |
|---|---|---|---|
| ____ accountable (w) | ____ driver (w) | ____ likes change (x) | ____ responsible (w) |
| ____ accuracy (z) | ____ dutiful (w) | ____ link together (y) | ____ results oriented (w) |
| ____ achievement (w) | ____ efficient (w) | ____ listening (y) | ____ risk taker (x) |
| ____ adventurer (x) | ____ emotional (y) | ____ literal (z) | ____ romantic (y) |
| ____ agreeable (y) | ____ enthusiastic (x) | ____ logical (z) | ____ saving (w) |
| ____ amiable (y) | ____ exacting (z) | ____ loving (y) | ____ sensitive (y) |
| ____ analytical (z) | ____ excitable (x) | ____ loyal (y) | ____ sentimental (y) |
| ____ asks (y) | ____ exciting (x) | ____ mastery (z) | ____ serious (z) |
| ____ authority (w) | ____ fast (x) | ____ mover (x) | ____ skeptical (z) |
| ____ avoids conflict (y) | ____ feelings first (y) | ____ orderly (z) | ____ spends (x) |
| ____ being accepted (y) | ____ flamboyant (x) | ____ organized (z) | ____ spontaneous (x) |
| ____ being in control (w) | ____ flashy (x) | ____ originality (x) | ____ spurt worker (x) |
| ____ bottom line (w) | ____ flexible (x) | ____ patient (z) | ____ status (w) |
| ____ budgets (z) | ____ freedom (x) | ____ people centered (y) | ____ stimulating (x) |
| ____ careful (z) | ____ friendly (y) | ____ perfectionist (z) | ____ strategist (z) |
| ____ cautious action (z) | ____ fun (x) | ____ performer (x) | ____ strong-willed (w) |
| ____ challenge authority (x) | ____ future focus (x) | ____ planner (z) | ____ structure (w) |
| ____ conceptual (z) | ____ gestures (x) | ____ playful (x) | ____ supportive (y) |
| ____ conforming (y) | ____ giving (y) | ____ powerful (w) | ____ sympathetic (y) |
| ____ considerate (y) | ____ harmonious (y) | ____ practical (w) | ____ take charge (w) |
| ____ creative (x) | ____ helps others (y) | ____ precise (z) | ____ team oriented (y) |
| ____ decisive (w) | ____ history (z) | ____ predicts (z) | ____ tells (w) |
| ____ demanding (w) | ____ honest feelings (y) | ____ prepared (w) | ____ theoretical (z) |
| ____ dependable (y) | ____ impatient (w) | ____ present focused (y) | ____ thinker (z) |
| ____ detail oriented (z) | ____ implementer (w) | ____ prioritizes (z) | ____ tough (w) |
| ____ direct (w) | ____ impulsive (x) | ____ probing (z) | ____ traditional (w) |
| ____ discipline (w) | ____ innovative (z) | ____ quality (z) | ____ warmth (y) |
| ____ do it now (w) | ____ law & order (w) | ____ questioning (z) | ____ willing (y) |
| ____ down with routine (x) | ____ leader (w) | ____ rapid reaction (x) | ____ works best alone (z) |
| ____ dramatic (x) | ____ lighthearted (x) | ____ relater (y) | ____ zestful (x) |

____ "z" words  ____ "y" words  ____ "x" words  ____ "w" words

Total up the number of checks you've placed next to words with the "w," "x," "y" or "z" notation. Refer to chapter 3, page 38 in *Success Signals* for the KEY to this Profile.

# Success Signals Profile

INSTRUCTIONS: Place a check by each word that is **really** like you. If the meaning of the word is unclear, do not place a check by it. After you've completed the Profile, turn the page upside down to tally your score.

| | | | |
|---|---|---|---|
| ___ accountable (w) | ___ driver (w) | ___ likes change (x) | ___ responsible (w) |
| ___ accuracy (z) | ___ dutiful (w) | ___ link together (y) | ___ results oriented (w) |
| ___ achievement (w) | ___ efficient (w) | ___ listening (y) | ___ risk taker (x) |
| ___ adventurer (x) | ___ emotional (y) | ___ literal (z) | ___ romantic (y) |
| ___ agreeable (y) | ___ enthusiastic (x) | ___ logical (z) | ___ saving (w) |
| ___ amiable (y) | ___ exacting (z) | ___ loving (y) | ___ sensitive (y) |
| ___ analytical (z) | ___ excitable (x) | ___ loyal (y) | ___ sentimental (y) |
| ___ asks (y) | ___ exciting (x) | ___ mastery (z) | ___ serious (z) |
| ___ authority (w) | ___ fast (x) | ___ mover (x) | ___ skeptical (z) |
| ___ avoids conflict (y) | ___ feelings first (y) | ___ orderly (z) | ___ spends (x) |
| ___ being accepted (y) | ___ flamboyant (x) | ___ organized (z) | ___ spontaneous (x) |
| ___ being in control (w) | ___ flashy (x) | ___ originality (x) | ___ spurt worker (x) |
| ___ bottom line (w) | ___ flexible (x) | ___ patient (z) | ___ status (w) |
| ___ budgets (z) | ___ freedom (x) | ___ people centered (y) | ___ stimulating (x) |
| ___ careful (z) | ___ friendly (y) | ___ perfectionist (z) | ___ strategist (z) |
| ___ cautious action (z) | ___ fun (x) | ___ performer (x) | ___ strong-willed (w) |
| ___ challenge authority (x) | ___ future focus (x) | ___ planner (z) | ___ structure (w) |
| ___ conceptual (z) | ___ gestures (x) | ___ playful (x) | ___ supportive (y) |
| ___ conforming (y) | ___ giving (y) | ___ powerful (w) | ___ sympathetic (y) |
| ___ considerate (y) | ___ harmonious (y) | ___ practical (w) | ___ take charge (w) |
| ___ creative (x) | ___ helps others (y) | ___ precise (z) | ___ team oriented (y) |
| ___ decisive (w) | ___ history (z) | ___ predicts (z) | ___ tells (w) |
| ___ demanding (w) | ___ honest feelings (y) | ___ prepared (w) | ___ theoretical (z) |
| ___ dependable (y) | ___ impatient (w) | ___ present focused (y) | ___ thinker (z) |
| ___ detail oriented (z) | ___ implementer (w) | ___ prioritizes (z) | ___ tough (w) |
| ___ direct (w) | ___ impulsive (x) | ___ probing (z) | ___ traditional (w) |
| ___ discipline (w) | ___ innovative (z) | ___ quality (z) | ___ warmth (y) |
| ___ do it now (w) | ___ law & order (w) | ___ questioning (z) | ___ willing (y) |
| ___ down with routine (x) | ___ leader (w) | ___ rapid reaction (x) | ___ works best alone (z) |
| ___ dramatic (x) | ___ lighthearted (x) | ___ relater (y) | ___ zestful (x) |

Total up the number of checks you've placed next to words with the "w," "x," "y" or "z" notation. Refer to chapter 3, page 38 in *Success Signals* for the KEY to this Profile.

___ "w" words     ___ "x" words     ___ "y" words     ___ "z" words

# Success Signals Profile

INSTRUCTIONS: Place a check by each word that is **really** like you. If the meaning of the word is unclear, do not place a check by it. After you've completed the Profile, turn the page upside down to tally your score.

| | | | |
|---|---|---|---|
| ____ accountable (w) | ____ driver (w) | ____ likes change (x) | ____ responsible (w) |
| ____ accuracy (z) | ____ dutiful (w) | ____ link together (y) | ____ results oriented (w) |
| ____ achievement (w) | ____ efficient (w) | ____ listening (y) | ____ risk taker (x) |
| ____ adventurer (x) | ____ emotional (y) | ____ literal (z) | ____ romantic (y) |
| ____ agreeable (y) | ____ enthusiastic (x) | ____ logical (z) | ____ saving (w) |
| ____ amiable (y) | ____ exacting (z) | ____ loving (y) | ____ sensitive (y) |
| ____ analytical (z) | ____ excitable (x) | ____ loyal (y) | ____ sentimental (y) |
| ____ asks (y) | ____ exciting (x) | ____ mastery (z) | ____ serious (z) |
| ____ authority (w) | ____ fast (x) | ____ mover (x) | ____ skeptical (z) |
| ____ avoids conflict (y) | ____ feelings first (y) | ____ orderly (z) | ____ spends (x) |
| ____ being accepted (y) | ____ flamboyant (x) | ____ organized (z) | ____ spontaneous (x) |
| ____ being in control (w) | ____ flashy (x) | ____ originality (x) | ____ spurt worker (x) |
| ____ bottom line (w) | ____ flexible (x) | ____ patient (z) | ____ status (w) |
| ____ budgets (z) | ____ freedom (x) | ____ people centered (y) | ____ stimulating (x) |
| ____ careful (z) | ____ friendly (y) | ____ perfectionist (z) | ____ strategist (z) |
| ____ cautious action (z) | ____ fun (x) | ____ performer (x) | ____ strong-willed (w) |
| ____ challenge authority (x) | ____ future focus (x) | ____ planner (z) | ____ structure (w) |
| ____ conceptual (z) | ____ gestures (x) | ____ playful (x) | ____ supportive (y) |
| ____ conforming (y) | ____ giving (y) | ____ powerful (w) | ____ sympathetic (y) |
| ____ considerate (y) | ____ harmonious (y) | ____ practical (w) | ____ take charge (w) |
| ____ creative (x) | ____ helps others (y) | ____ precise (z) | ____ team oriented (y) |
| ____ decisive (w) | ____ history (z) | ____ predicts (z) | ____ tells (w) |
| ____ demanding (w) | ____ honest feelings (y) | ____ prepared (w) | ____ theoretical (z) |
| ____ dependable (y) | ____ impatient (w) | ____ present focused (y) | ____ thinker (z) |
| ____ detail oriented (z) | ____ implementer (w) | ____ prioritizes (z) | ____ tough (w) |
| ____ direct (w) | ____ impulsive (x) | ____ probing (z) | ____ traditional (w) |
| ____ discipline (w) | ____ innovative (z) | ____ quality (z) | ____ warmth (y) |
| ____ do it now (w) | ____ law & order (w) | ____ questioning (z) | ____ willing (y) |
| ____ down with routine (x) | ____ leader (w) | ____ rapid reaction (x) | ____ works best alone (z) |
| ____ dramatic (x) | ____ lighthearted (x) | ____ relater (y) | ____ zestful (x) |

____ "z" words      ____ "y" words      ____ "x" words      ____ "w" words

Total up the number of checks you've placed next to words with the "w," "x," "y," or "z" notation. Refer to chapter 3, page 38 in *Success Signals* for the KEY to this Profile.

# Success Signals Profile

INSTRUCTIONS: Place a check by each word that is **really** like you. If the meaning of the word is unclear, do not place a check by it. After you've completed the Profile, turn the page upside down to tally your score.

| | | | |
|---|---|---|---|
| ___ accountable (w) | ___ driver (w) | ___ likes change (x) | ___ responsible (w) |
| ___ accuracy (z) | ___ dutiful (w) | ___ link together (y) | ___ results oriented (w) |
| ___ achievement (w) | ___ efficient (w) | ___ listening (y) | ___ risk taker (x) |
| ___ adventurer (x) | ___ emotional (y) | ___ literal (z) | ___ romantic (y) |
| ___ agreeable (y) | ___ enthusiastic (x) | ___ logical (z) | ___ saving (w) |
| ___ amiable (y) | ___ exacting (z) | ___ loving (y) | ___ sensitive (y) |
| ___ analytical (z) | ___ excitable (x) | ___ loyal (y) | ___ sentimental (y) |
| ___ asks (y) | ___ exciting (x) | ___ mastery (z) | ___ serious (z) |
| ___ authority (w) | ___ fast (x) | ___ mover (x) | ___ skeptical (z) |
| ___ avoids conflict (y) | ___ feelings first (y) | ___ orderly (z) | ___ spends (x) |
| ___ being accepted (y) | ___ flamboyant (x) | ___ organized (z) | ___ spontaneous (x) |
| ___ being in control (w) | ___ flashy (x) | ___ originality (x) | ___ spurt worker (x) |
| ___ bottom line (w) | ___ flexible (x) | ___ patient (z) | ___ status (w) |
| ___ budgets (z) | ___ freedom (x) | ___ people centered (y) | ___ stimulating (x) |
| ___ careful (z) | ___ friendly (y) | ___ perfectionist (z) | ___ strategist (z) |
| ___ cautious action (z) | ___ fun (x) | ___ performer (x) | ___ strong-willed (w) |
| ___ challenge authority (x) | ___ future focus (x) | ___ planner (z) | ___ structure (w) |
| ___ conceptual (z) | ___ gestures (x) | ___ playful (x) | ___ supportive (y) |
| ___ conforming (y) | ___ giving (y) | ___ powerful (w) | ___ sympathetic (y) |
| ___ considerate (y) | ___ harmonious (y) | ___ practical (w) | ___ take charge (w) |
| ___ creative (x) | ___ helps others (y) | ___ precise (z) | ___ team oriented (y) |
| ___ decisive (w) | ___ history (z) | ___ predicts (z) | ___ tells (w) |
| ___ demanding (w) | ___ honest feelings (y) | ___ prepared (w) | ___ theoretical (z) |
| ___ dependable (y) | ___ impatient (w) | ___ present focused (y) | ___ thinker (z) |
| ___ detail oriented (z) | ___ implementer (w) | ___ prioritizes (z) | ___ tough (w) |
| ___ direct (w) | ___ impulsive (x) | ___ probing (z) | ___ traditional (w) |
| ___ discipline (w) | ___ innovative (z) | ___ quality (z) | ___ warmth (y) |
| ___ do it now (w) | ___ law & order (w) | ___ questioning (z) | ___ willing (y) |
| ___ down with routine (x) | ___ leader (w) | ___ rapid reaction (x) | ___ works best alone (z) |
| ___ dramatic (x) | ___ lighthearted (x) | ___ relater (y) | ___ zestful (x) |

___ "w" words     ___ "x" words     ___ "y" words     ___ "z" words

Total up the number of checks you've placed next to words with the "w," "x," "y" or "z" notation. Refer to chapter 3, page 38 in *Success Signals* for the KEY to this Profile.

Agreement Dynamics • P.O. Box 33640, Seattle, WA 98133 • U.S.A.

www.agreementdynamics.com
Phone: (206) 546-8048

# Success Signals Profile

INSTRUCTIONS: Place a check by each word that is **really** like you. If the meaning of the word is unclear, do not place a check by it. After you've completed the Profile, turn the page upside down to tally your score.

| | | | |
|---|---|---|---|
| _____ accountable (w) | _____ driver (w) | _____ likes change (x) | _____ responsible (w) |
| _____ accuracy (z) | _____ dutiful (w) | _____ link together (y) | _____ results oriented (w) |
| _____ achievement (w) | _____ efficient (w) | _____ listening (y) | _____ risk taker (x) |
| _____ adventurer (x) | _____ emotional (y) | _____ literal (z) | _____ romantic (y) |
| _____ agreeable (y) | _____ enthusiastic (x) | _____ logical (z) | _____ saving (w) |
| _____ amiable (y) | _____ exacting (z) | _____ loving (y) | _____ sensitive (y) |
| _____ analytical (z) | _____ excitable (x) | _____ loyal (y) | _____ sentimental (y) |
| _____ asks (y) | _____ exciting (x) | _____ mastery (z) | _____ serious (z) |
| _____ authority (w) | _____ fast (x) | _____ mover (x) | _____ skeptical (z) |
| _____ avoids conflict (y) | _____ feelings first (y) | _____ orderly (z) | _____ spends (x) |
| _____ being accepted (y) | _____ flamboyant (x) | _____ organized (z) | _____ spontaneous (x) |
| _____ being in control (w) | _____ flashy (x) | _____ originality (x) | _____ spurt worker (x) |
| _____ bottom line (w) | _____ flexible (x) | _____ patient (z) | _____ status (w) |
| _____ budgets (z) | _____ freedom (x) | _____ people centered (y) | _____ stimulating (x) |
| _____ careful (z) | _____ friendly (y) | _____ perfectionist (z) | _____ strategist (z) |
| _____ cautious action (z) | _____ fun (x) | _____ performer (x) | _____ strong-willed (w) |
| _____ challenge authority (x) | _____ future focus (x) | _____ planner (z) | _____ structure (w) |
| _____ conceptual (z) | _____ gestures (x) | _____ playful (x) | _____ supportive (y) |
| _____ conforming (y) | _____ giving (y) | _____ powerful (w) | _____ sympathetic (y) |
| _____ considerate (y) | _____ harmonious (y) | _____ practical (w) | _____ take charge (w) |
| _____ creative (x) | _____ helps others (y) | _____ precise (z) | _____ team oriented (y) |
| _____ decisive (w) | _____ history (z) | _____ predicts (z) | _____ tells (w) |
| _____ demanding (w) | _____ honest feelings (y) | _____ prepared (w) | _____ theoretical (z) |
| _____ dependable (y) | _____ impatient (w) | _____ present focused (y) | _____ thinker (z) |
| _____ detail oriented (z) | _____ implementer (w) | _____ prioritizes (z) | _____ tough (w) |
| _____ direct (w) | _____ impulsive (x) | _____ probing (z) | _____ traditional (w) |
| _____ discipline (w) | _____ innovative (z) | _____ quality (z) | _____ warmth (y) |
| _____ do it now (w) | _____ law & order (w) | _____ questioning (z) | _____ willing (y) |
| _____ down with routine (x) | _____ leader (w) | _____ rapid reaction (x) | _____ works best alone (z) |
| _____ dramatic (x) | _____ lighthearted (x) | _____ relater (y) | _____ zestful (x) |

Total up the number of checks you've placed next to words with the "w," "x," "y," or "z" notation. Refer to chapter 3, page 38 in *Success Signals* for the KEY to this Profile.

_____ "w" words   _____ "x" words   _____ "y" words   _____ "z" words

# Products from Agreement Dynamics

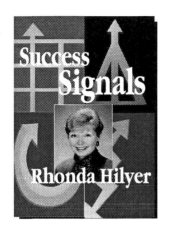

## SUCCESS SIGNALS VHS FORMAT          $29.95

Aired on public television stations, this is an important addition to your Success Signals library, and can enrich your communication in immediate and lasting ways. The program's author, Rhonda Hilyer, presents this highly acclaimed workshop in front of a live studio audience. Powerful and practical approaches to success with others are presented with compelling examples, wit and humor. Order your copy today.

## TRUST AND RESPECT AUDIO TAPE    $13.95

This audio tape, by Rhonda Hilyer, provides tools to build trust between individuals. Her engaging and humorous discussion looks at reality checks, respect, and esteem-building behaviors.

## ANGER TOOLS AUDIO TAPE            $13.95

This audio tape, by Rhonda Hilyer, provides insight into the types of anger we encounter, when anger can be appropriate, how to defuse our own anger and that of others and how to overcome chronic anger.

TURN TO THE NEXT PAGE TO ORDER ADDITIONAL
COPIES OF THE *SUCCESS SIGNALS* BOOK AND
THESE AGREEMENT DYNAMICS PRODUCTS.

# Agreement Dynamics Product Order Form

To order Agreement Dynamics products, please complete the following form, include your check made payable to "Agreement Dynamics," and mail your order to the address shown below.

Name _____

Address _____

_____

City                    State            Zip Code            Tel. Number

| Product | Quantity | Price | Amount |
|---|---|---|---|
| Success Signals VIDEO | | $29.95 | |
| *Success Signals* (book & color cards) | | $29.95 | |
| Trust and Respect audio tape | | $13.95 | |
| Anger Tools audio tape | | $13.95 | |

### SHIPPING RATES:

*Allow 5-7 days to receive orders*

For orders 0-$100          Add $6.50

For orders $101-$200       Add $9.75

*For rush shipping or orders over $201, please call Agreement Dynamics for rates 1-800-97-AGREE*

| | Amount |
|---|---|
| ORDER SUBTOTAL | |
| Sales Tax: Washington residents Multiply the Subtotal x .088 OR add $2.64 per book or video ordered; $1.23 per audio tape | |
| Shipping and Handling (see shipping rates) | |
| GRAND TOTAL | |

**TO ORDER: Complete this form, include check with your GRAND TOTAL made to "Agreement Dynamics" and send to: ADI, PO Box 33640, Seattle, WA 98133**

**For questions: Call 1-800-97-AGREE**